DIVORCE MATTERS

WHAT YOU REALLY NEED TO KNOW WHEN IT'S TIME TO GET A DIVORCE

KATHY CRISCUOLO BOUFFORD, ESQ

The information and advice contained in this book are based upon the research and professional experience of the author, but it is important to note that divorce law may vary from state to state. Please be sure to consult a divorce attorney or divorce-related organization in your state for information applicable to your case.

Typesetting and cover design: Gary A. Rosenberg

Square One Publishers
115 Herricks Road
Garden City Park, NY 11040
(516) 535-2010 • (877) 900-BOOK
www.squareonepublishers.com

Library of Congress Cataloging-in-Publication Data

Names: Criscuolo Boufford, Kathy, author.
Title: Divorce matters / Kathy Criscuolo Boufford.
Description: Garden City Park : Square One Publishers, 2024. | Includes bibliographical references and index.
Identifiers: LCCN 2023037943 (print) | LCCN 2023037944 (ebook) | ISBN 9780757005251 (paperback) | ISBN 9780757055256 (ebook)
Subjects: LCSH: Divorce—Law and legislation—United States. | Separation (Law)—United States. | Custody of children—United States. | Husband and wife—United States.
Classification: LCC KF535 .B59 2024 (print) | LCC KF535 (ebook) | DDC 346.7301/66—dc23/eng/20230928
LC record available at https://lccn.loc.gov/2023037943
LC ebook record available at https://lccn.loc.gov/2023037944

Copyright © 2024 by Kathy Criscuolo Boufford

All rights reserved. No part of this publication may be reproduced, scanned, uploaded, stored in a retrieval system, or transmitted, in any form or by any means, electronic, mechanical, photocopying, recording, or otherwise, without the prior written permission of the publisher.

Contents

Acknowledgments, v

Preface, vii

Introduction, 1

1. First Steps, 3

2. Consulting an Attorney, 17

3. Preparation, 31

4. Discovery, 43

5. Getting a Friendly Divorce, 51

6. Regarding Children, 67

7. Money Matters, 87

8. Negotiation, Settlement, and Trial, 113

9. Abuse, Addiction, and Mental Illness, 131

10. Life after Divorce, 145

Conclusion, 161

Glossary, 163

Resources, 169

About the Author, 173

Index, 175

Acknowledgments

First and foremost, I'd like to thank and recognize my current and former clients, especially those who took the time to provide me with their thoughts on what information was most helpful, what they had learned through the divorce process, and what they thought would be of assistance to those starting the process. The trust and confidence you place in me is fully appreciated and what drives me to do my best every day.

Thank you to my business partner, attorney Ronald K. Bellenot, Sr., and all current and former team members at Bellenot & Boufford, LLC. It takes at least two to three people to prepare me to do what I need to do and be where I need to be at any given time. I expect a lot from you all, and you consistently deliver to the betterment of our clients. I could not do it without your help.

Thank you to my initial editor and writing counsel, Christine Thom of Stardust Editorial. You offered so much more than your technical assistance, and I am grateful to have found you. You saw this book's potential and encouraged me to seek out publishers. You were right.

Thank you to Rudy Shur of Square One Publishers. You took a chance on working with a trial attorney—a job not for the faint of heart. You were extremely patient with my schedule. During our long talks you were continually able to tease out more content and help me to see the material from a non-lawyer perspective. This project was truly a joint venture, with each of us staying in our own lanes. I really enjoyed working with you.

And last but not least, thank you to my family. Your support means everything. I am very lucky to have you all in my life.

Preface

For the majority of people going through it, divorce is not an easy time. Those facing a divorce experience a great deal of emotional upheaval. A majority of my time as an attorney is spent practicing divorce and family law, so I know all too well that a spouse's decision to end a marriage can take a great toll on both parties. Spouses who decide to divorce often worry about how the divorce is going to affect them, their children, and their day to day lives. They must also deal with all the powerful emotions surrounding the breakdown of their marriage. It is a difficult area of practice for attorneys. Nevertheless, I genuinely appreciate the opportunity to assist those going through this process. I am humbled by the trust they put in me, and this trust drives me to do my very best to represent them in litigation or guide them through mediation. I try to leave clients and their children in a better situation than when they first came to me. At the end of the day, a job well done frequently leaves me a little battle worn and weary, but with a happy heart and a grateful client.

My experience with a client's divorce typically starts with a phone call—someone on the other end who has either been served with court papers or is thinking about starting a legal action. This person is happy to be able to get some quick answers regarding divorce procedures and costs in a brief conversation over the phone. It's scary to contact an attorney, so I try to make the caller feel comfortable talking with me. I quickly dispel some of the misinformation the caller may have gotten and assure them that their worst fears will likely not come to pass. What I have come to learn is that providing a client with the correct information up front and throughout the process helps them to understand what they have to do and empowers them to do so.

As different as each case is, people generally have the same initial concerns and questions when beginning the divorce process. The information they need is consistent. This fact has allowed me to write articles and lecture on the topic of divorce, providing answers to the most common questions about divorce. During one of my presentations, I was asked by someone in the audience if I had written a book on the subject. This was not the first time I had been asked this question. While my answer was no, this time it got me thinking. What if I could make a lot of information easily available to assist those thinking about or going through a divorce? It would hopefully make the process less overwhelming. It would prepare people for what was to come. It would help them become better participants and advocates for themselves. Inspired by the prospect of making a difficult time a little less difficult for more people than I ever could by simply answering the phone, I decided to write this book.

Introduction

Divorce is an overwhelming prospect for most. There are so many questions and uncertainties involved. Yet thousands of people file for divorce each day. Where do they start? Most people begin by getting information about the process of filing for divorce. Becoming informed is beneficial and usually reduces anxiety in the long run. We humans tend to be frightened of unknowns—the times when we have to face the monster under the bed. Most people find the undertaking of divorce to be one of these times.

When people are contemplating divorce, some will go straight to an attorney, but most will first try to conduct their own research on the subject through friends, family, the internet, or other outside sources. It's important to point out that there is a lot of bad information on divorce out there. I know this fact only too well. As a family law attorney, I've been representing men and women going through divorce for close to three decades. I also mediate divorces for spouses going through the mediation process.

This book was written with you in mind. It provides high-quality practical information without bias in an easy and approachable format. I have seen so many instances in which access to a little bit of correct information could have gone a long way in saving someone from a lot of hardship. Perhaps a better decision would have been made or an action would not have been taken had only this information been received. It is almost always harder and more expensive to "walk back" a divorce-related decision than it is to get it right the first time. I've heard divorced spouses say, "I wish I'd known that," or, "I should have talked to you before," one too many times.

Although there seems to be a lot of books about post-divorce life available, I have not seen much good information out there for people who are going through—or who are about to go through—the process of divorce. A small survey I conducted with some of my past clients revealed that they would have welcomed this type of information to both prepare them for the process prior to hiring me and to assist them in working with me.

While the laws and procedures regarding divorce can vary from state to state, the information found in this book can help any American who is facing divorce. Each chapter provides you with an overview of a divorce-related subject as well as guidance based on my years of experience. Chapter 1 discusses the practical issues to think about when beginning the process of divorce, while Chapter 2 explains what type of attorney you might need and how to find the right professional to hire. Chapters 3 and 4 then describe how to prepare for your case and detail all the elements you may be required to provide.

Chapter 5 strikes a hopeful note by showing how couples can have a "friendly divorce" by bypassing traditional litigation and getting divorced through mediation. Chapter 6 talks about all the crucial considerations associated with divorces that involve children, while Chapter 7 goes over a common source of contention in divorce: money matters. Chapter 8 then outlines the process of negotiation, settlement, and trial. Chapter 9 is dedicated to offering guidance on how to manage your response when you are divorcing a spouse who may be abusive, an addict, or struggling with mental illness. Finally, Chapter 10 teaches you how to pave the way for your post-divorce life.

This book is sure to validate or allow you to dismiss some of your concerns regarding divorce. Ultimately, it is meant to prevent you from making common mistakes and point you in the right direction. Having this information at hand is likely to save you some heartache, time, and money.

I am not a proponent of divorce. In fact, I think all efforts should be made to save a marriage. I do realize, however, that despite people's best efforts, some marriages cannot, or should not, remain intact. I understand that some marriages are unhealthy or even dangerous. The decision to end your marriage is yours (or your spouse's) to make, not mine or any other attorney's. Once you arrive at the point of beginning a divorce, whether voluntarily or not, it's my job to give you the information you need to see it through successfully. Knowledge is power, and with this power comes the confidence to move forward and make the best out of a bad situation. Divorce is a heavy burden, but knowing what you can expect to face during the process will make it seem lighter.

1.

First Steps

The decision to dissolve a marriage is not an easy one. Maybe you have been thinking about it for many years, or perhaps something occurred recently to set the wheels in motion. There are many possible reasons, of course, for your staying in a bad marriage. You may have stayed in your marriage for financial reasons. You may have stayed for the sake of your children. Maybe your religious beliefs have motivated you to stay married, or maybe you have been worried about how divorce might make you look to your family and friends. Maybe you and your spouse have lived separate lives for years, doing your own things with your kids, attending social functions and holiday gatherings apart, sleeping in separate rooms, and mutually acknowledging your loss of interest in each other.

On the other hand, you may have thought you were happily married only to find out your partner does not feel the same. You may have found out that your spouse has been cheating on you, perhaps for years. You may be faced with the additional burden of having an abusive spouse or a spouse with substance abuse issues. Regardless of what has brought you to the point of wanting to get a divorce and thus end your marriage, it is a very big decision, the consequences of which are likely to be far-reaching and experienced by not only you but also your loved ones. It is therefore important to think about and prepare yourself for all the changes that are about to take place in your life.

COMMON CONCERNS

When considering a divorce, you are likely to encounter many concerns about how the divorce will affect you, your family, and even your friends. In other words, you will worry about the impacts divorce can have on every aspect of your life. The longer the marriage and the more intertwined a couple's lives are, the harder it is to overcome these worries. These fears may prevent you from moving forward with your divorce, or from adequately responding to a divorce initiated by your spouse. It is important to understand that this apprehension is natural. There will be a lot of questions and uncertainties that arise at the beginning of your divorce.

Initially, it is unlikely that you will know what the terms of your divorce will be, and you may not even know what you would like the end result of your divorce to look like. Your attorney will need a good deal of information before being able to give you any strong sense of what you might expect. For now, here are some things that will come up that should not be a surprise, some of which you may have already thought about.

Money

The financial reality of ultimately supporting two households instead of one after your divorce can be extremely daunting. Most spouses commingle their financial assets and plan to fund their future together, sharing expenses. Now you are facing the prospect of dividing your assets and increasing your expenses. Furthermore, family planning decisions made long ago may have negatively affected your or your spouse's earning capacity or career advancement. Perhaps you are unfamiliar with the family finances, or worse, have no access to the family finances. In addition, you are probably unsure of the fees involved in hiring an attorney and in the dark about how much the divorce process will ultimately cost. These are real concerns about matters that will affect your immediate and future finances. While it may not be easy to accept, it is important to consider the economic impact that divorce will have on your life. Here are the most common questions to keep in mind:

- How will our assets be divided?
- How will I support myself?
- Can we afford two households?
- Will I have to get a job right away?
- How much alimony will I have to pay?

FIRST STEPS

- How much child support am I entitled to?
- How do I obtain financial information?
- Can I get access to money before the divorce?
- How much will hiring a lawyer cost?
- How much does a divorce usually cost?

Living Arrangements

Most spouses are still living together at the time the divorce starts. If you get along with your spouse or have different schedules and contact is at a minimum, continuing to share the house during the divorce process may pose little issue for you. You may have already decided on separate sleeping arrangements and are respectful of each other's privacy and space.

On the other hand, you may find living together extremely uncomfortable and wish for nothing more than to separate physically during the divorce process. You and your spouse may simply wish to live separately but disagree on who should leave the house. Even if you both remain in the home, the pending divorce will necessarily change the dynamics of the living situation between you and your spouse. It may make it better; it may make it worse.

Your children will be affected no matter what, having to navigate your changing relationship and any adjustment in their living circumstances. They may have to go between houses to spend time with each parent prior to the finalization of your divorce, provided you and your spouse plan on living apart during this time. This is not an easy subject to manage, and you should prepare for it by considering the following questions:

- Can my spouse and I continue to live together while our divorce is pending?
- Do I have to move out of the house right away?
- Can I force my spouse to move out of the house?
- If I move out, where will I live?
- If I move out, is that considered abandonment?

- If I move out, will I lose my house?
- How will the marital home expenses be paid during the divorce?
- What will happen with the children if I live separately from my spouse?

Childcare

Raising children in separate households pre- and post-divorce can be a challenge even in the best of scenarios. It is perfectly normal to worry about how divorce may affect your children as well as your relationship with them. This may be especially relevant if you and your spouse have different styles of parenting and frequently argued about how to parent your children. Of course, your concerns may go further in this matter. You may question the ability or fitness of your spouse to parent adequately without your being there. Practically speaking, your parenting time after divorce might necessitate changes in your work schedule or childcare assistance. You may wonder or worry about how and when your child can be introduced to a significant other. You may be concerned about a third party, such as a new romantic partner of your spouse, supervising or even parenting your children. The following questions should be kept in mind as the process moves forward:

- How is custody typically decided?
- If I move out of the home, when will I see my children?
- What are the most common parenting arrangements?
- What will holidays be like?
- Will my children have to change schools if I am granted custody but have moved out of the home?
- How will decisions be made for my children if my spouse and I disagree?
- Can my child's wishes be made known to the judge?

Family Relationships

Once a divorce starts, it is hard for family members not to take sides. You may worry about your ability to trust certain people with whom you have been very close prior to the divorce. How might your relationship with these people change? How will holidays and other family events be attended during the divorce process? Maybe you are worried that you will be made to look bad in front of your spouse's family. If you share children with your spouse, you may be concerned about what might be said about you to them or simply in front of them. You may wonder what your children are saying to your spouse or your spouse's family in your absence. It is therefore important to be aware of the impact that family dynamics may have on this situation.

Friends

Like family members, friends may play a big part of your married life. Many spouses have shared social circles and mutual friends. If you have young children, often your associations revolve around your children's friends and activities. It is reasonable to wonder what might become of these friendships. Will certain people stop associating with you because you are no longer with your spouse? Will they treat you differently? Will they take sides or talk behind your back? Will they tell your spouse things you have said to them in confidence? Unfortunately, people do take sides, so you should prepare to recognize which of your friends you can count on.

Stress

Your divorce will likely weigh heavily on you. After all, it involves terminating a relationship that in all likelihood started out well, one that you did not plan on ending. If you've been married longer than you have been single, being someone's spouse has become part of your identity. So many of your memories probably involve your spouse in some way, shape, or form. All this is to say that divorce will not be an easy adjustment to make. You will likely experience some strong emotions during your divorce, including guilt, sadness, anger, and relief. You may find it hard to control these emotions and sometimes you may not even want to try to do so. You may unwittingly take your feelings out on others. In addition to having to face all the divorce-related issues already discussed, you also have the additional burden of dealing with the "nuts and bolts" of the divorce process, such as finding an attorney. It's no wonder you may be feeling overwhelmed.

Once the decision to divorce has been made, there often arises an immediate urge to get the legal process started. At the same time, a heightened anxiety about the divorce process and its end results also tends to take hold. It's almost as though you are getting ready to walk through fire. You want to get it over with, but you are also worried about the shape you will be in after you've done it. It's common to be at once laser-focused yet scatterbrained, relieved yet terrified, happy yet sad. It's normal to have lots of questions, to want to talk and have someone understand you and tell you it's going to be okay. When you are prepared to face the challenges ahead, you will know it's going to be okay—even if you do have to walk through fire.

Your first challenge will be finding the right attorney. Once an attorney is representing you, your stress level should come down. You may still be worried or have periods of high anxiety, but knowing you have a knowledgeable advocate on your side should be reassuring. Be aware

The Importance of Self-Care

It is incredibly easy to spend all of your waking hours (and even some of your sleeping hours) worrying about the dissolution of your marriage. The consequences of doing so, however, can be dire and affect not only yourself but those you care about. Constant worrying can have a negative effect on your well-being. It's common to start eating poorly and sleeping poorly, depriving your body of the energy and rest it needs to function and stay healthy. Without maintaining a proper diet and sleeping well, your ability to concentrate and maintain a balanced mood will suffer, and you will be prone to getting sick. Your failing health may then have a negative effect on your relationships and employment—a lack of concentration often leads to mistakes and forgetfulness, and irritability can lead to (often unnecessary) arguments and even result in irresponsible behavior. Sickness can also impair your ability to take care of your children.

It is imperative that you take care of yourself. In order to do so, you need to release stress and find some happiness and peace. It is not selfish for you to acknowledge this fact. How you take care of yourself and cope with stress will be unique to you, of course.

that different attorneys can be experienced in different aspects of the law. Typically, an attorney will limit their law practice to a certain area of the law, similar to a doctor who specializes in treating a certain body part or in performing a particular procedure. Ideally, you will want to find an attorney who has a lot of experience representing people in divorce proceedings. But where do you start?

FINDING A DIVORCE ATTORNEY

When first looking for a divorce attorney, it is important to know that most attorneys who represent people in divorce matters advertise their work as being in *family law* and refer to themselves as "family law attorneys." Most people assume that family law attorneys handle the drafting of end-of-life documents (e.g., last will and testament, living will, trust, etc.) and the administration of estates in probate court on

> Exercise, yoga, meditation, prayer, binge watching a favorite show, regular socialization that does not involve discussions about your divorce, and playing with animals are some of the healthy activities many of my clients have turned to with good results. In contrast, binge drinking and eating, as well as social media prowling of a soon-to-be ex are some of the unhealthy activities some of my clients have turned to, with very poor results.
>
> Being able to talk with family member or trusted friends may provide you with the help you need, but, unfortunately, some people find themselves, more or less, without friends or family. If you are one of these people, it is important to know that there are groups and organizations that hold meetings to help people who are going through such hard times in their lives. They may be sponsored by a religious organization or a secular therapeutic group. They will likely include people who have gone through what you are going through now. Do not be afraid to reach out to these groups to learn more about their services.
>
> Taking time for self-care won't necessarily make the divorce process any easier, but it will ease the negative consequences of stress that divorce often brings.

behalf of deceased estate owners. Matters such as these, however, fall under the domain of attorneys known as "trust and estate attorneys" or "probate attorneys."

While some issues overlap between types of lawyers, family law attorneys primarily handle matters related to the dissolution of a marriage as well as child custody and support, whether the parents were ever married or not. Specifically, family law representation includes divorce, legal separation, annulment, child custody and visitation, child support, contempt actions (penalties meant to enforce family court orders), and modification actions (petitions to change family court orders). Some family law attorneys may also call themselves "matrimonial attorneys" and use the term *matrimonial law* to describe the type of work they do. You shouldn't run into any problems in your search by simply referring to the attorney you are looking for as a divorce attorney.

Getting Leads

If you are comfortable talking about your situation with a family member or friend, you could ask this person for lawyer recommendations. A personal referral from someone who knows or has used a particular attorney—and was happy with the work that was done—is usually best. Of course, if you don't want your spouse to know you are seeking a divorce attorney, make sure the person you ask will keep this information confidential. If you've used an attorney for a different legal matter and found this person trustworthy, or if know an attorney through work that you like and trust, this attorney may also be a good referral source.

You can also conduct your own online search either before or after getting some referrals. Look at the content on a firm's website and see if it appeals to you. Read about its attorneys. Read reviews of the firm. Make a short list of questions based on the topics discussed in the next chapter and call the firm's office to schedule an initial consultation. After meeting with a prospective attorney, ask yourself the following questions:

- Did the attorney listen to you? Did you get the impression that your concerns were important to the attorney?

- Did the attorney answer your questions thoroughly?

- Did the attorney communicate in a way that made you feel both comfortable and confident in their understanding of the topics discussed?

FIRST STEPS

- Did the attorney offer you helpful information?
- Did the attorney explain how they communicate with their clients and who in their office will be available to assist you when they are in court or otherwise unavailable?
- Was the office staff helpful?
- Does the attorney have enough experience in divorce proceedings? How many years have they been representing people? How many cases have they handled? Would they be comfortable going to trial? What steps might they take to avoid trial? Would they be willing to negotiate hard?
- Is family law a primary area of the attorney's practice?
- Was the attorney up-front about fees and costs?
- Did the attorney indicate that you would be working as a team?
- Did the attorney ease your concerns?
- Did you feel comfortable talking with the attorney?

Only after speaking with an attorney will you be able to determine your comfort level with this person. You will be spending quite a bit of time with your divorce attorney during the process of divorce, and you will need to trust the advice of your divorce attorney as you make many important decisions along the way. It is imperative that you feel your voice is being heard, that the attorney will take the time to explain your options and answer your questions (repeatedly, if necessary), and that the attorney will be a strong advocate for you. In your first meeting, if an attorney does not exhibit compassion for you or seem enthusiastic to represent you, I strongly suggest you hire a different attorney.

Important Considerations

Here are some thoughts that may not be on the top of your mind, or which you may be reluctant to discuss with a prospective attorney. The qualities you would like to find in your divorce attorney, how much control you would like to have over the process, how much control you will have over the process, and the specifics of your divorce attorney's legal fees and billing are all subjects that should not be overlooked.

Finding a Good Fit

You are likely going to be working with your attorney quite a bit and doing so over an extended period of time during one of the most difficult times in your life. You want someone who is knowledgeable, strong, and experienced, no doubt. But you also want to feel comfortable with this person. What does this mean, exactly? What brings a person comfort? I think different things bring comfort to different people. For some, comfort comes from having confidence that certain results will be achieved. These people are perhaps not as concerned about the details or the process as others might be. They simply want to trust that the divorce will be taken care of within certain acceptable parameters. These people will be attracted to attorneys with a strong, confident presence. They will ask about their "track records" and "percentages," and they will gravitate towards attorneys who have achieved quantifiable, favorable results for their clients.

For others, comfort comes from having an emotional connection with an attorney and feeling that this attorney understands them. They will look for an attorney with empathy and welcome this attorney's ongoing guidance and support along the way. Then there are those who seek lots of information. For them, knowledge is power and, perhaps, a means to feel more in control, which brings them comfort. These people will look for an attorney who will provide them with vast amounts of written material, and who will spend lots of time explaining not only the process but also the various issues you should consider when making the numerous decisions you'll be asked to make throughout the course of a divorce case.

Think about and recognize what your preferences are and what your needs are going to be when choosing an attorney. Finding an attorney with the traits you are looking for will likely make you feel more confident and comfortable—and increase the chances of this attorney being a good fit for you.

Input and Control

When you hire an attorney, you are obviously seeking assistance with the legal aspects of your divorce. You are relying on your attorney's knowledge of the law and experience with the legal procedures that need to be followed to bring your case to a satisfactory resolution. There

FIRST STEPS

are several different ways in which a divorce case may proceed. Some cases progress slowly and methodically. Some cases move aggressively, with a flurry of activity. Some cases may be handled amicably, with a strong drive for settlement. And, of course, some cases are extremely combative.

Likewise, there are typically several ways in which to resolve a divorce, in regard to the particular terms that may be agreed upon or ordered by the court. In order for your attorney to guide and represent you properly and to your satisfaction, it is necessary for you to tell this attorney what you would like the result of your case to be, and how you would prefer your case to proceed. You will likely have some idea of what a good result might be—if not at the beginning of your case, then certainly after discussing it at length with your attorney. In addition, you will probably have a sense of how quickly or slowly your case might proceed. You may be prepared for, or even welcome, a long, drawn-out divorce. You may be looking forward to your day in court, hoping to present your case and perhaps obtain some retribution for perceived past wrongs.

You may, however, wish to reach a quick settlement and move on—either to hasten the official end of your marriage, get on with a new relationship, or minimize ongoing litigation for the sake of your children (and yourself). In a lengthy case, it may make sense to make all possible claims and negotiate hard, even if the other party might be hurt or angered by such actions. For the client seeking a speedy, amicable resolution, it may make sense to let a lot of claims go, or even offer more than a court might order.

It is important for your divorce attorney to be keenly aware of your goals and concerns, and to work with you to craft a unified approach to your case. While an attorney cannot control all aspects of a case, your attorney should at least strive to settle or fight the case according to your wishes. Communicating and strategizing with your attorney will be much easier if you have found someone who is a good fit.

Many decisions need to be made over the course of a divorce case. Which terms or positions are important and which are not, whether to agree to something or not, where to compromise, and how to proceed with the case at any given time are constant considerations. These decisions will be facilitated by your attorney based upon the facts and your attorney's experience, but they will ultimately be made by you. If your attorney does not agree with one of your decisions, you need to find out why this is. Your attorney should provide you with guidance in all legal matters relating to your divorce but should not undertake any legal actions without discussing them with you first.

Your attorney will almost certainly be more knowledgeable than you are when it comes to the law and legal procedure in relation to divorce. If you have a disagreement with your attorney, it is important to understand the reason for it. If your attorney is telling you that what you are seeking is unreasonable in light of the law, or that an argument you would like to make might hurt you, or that a procedural course you wish to pursue would be unwise, you need to seriously consider this advice. This is especially true when preparing for trial. You are not, however, obligated to take your attorney's advice. In fact, with few exceptions, your attorney is obligated to proceed as you wish.

It is important to consider and discuss with a prospective attorney the amount of input and control you can expect to have in your case. Be forthcoming about your preferences and expectations at the outset. You may expect to heed your attorney's advice in every circumstance, and that's fine, but you should be given the opportunity to consider and participate in any major decisions before they are made. A good attorney will confirm this understanding.

Cost and Type of Representation

Divorces come not only at an emotional cost but also a financial one. The amount you may pay for an attorney to assist you in your divorce can range from reasonably inexpensive to extremely expensive. It will largely depend upon the type and amount of legal assistance you require. You have choices—regarding not only the attorney you choose but also the work this attorney will do for you. (The different types of legal assistance available are discussed in detail in Chapter 2 on page 17.)

It is important for you to know that both *full representation* and *partial representation* exist. Full representation refers to what one usually thinks of when they think of hiring an attorney. This type of attorney will handle the entire legal matter for you. Partial representation, formally referred to as *limited scope representation,* involves you, the client, doing some of the work on your case while the attorney's work is limited to specific matters. Many people considering divorce are not able to afford to have an attorney represent them fully in their divorce cases. It is important to understand that you have the option of hiring an attorney to represent you partially, who will assist you only in certain aspects of your case.

Not surprisingly, the more involved your attorney is, the more legal fees you will incur. It should be pointed out, however, that any amount of money you might save by avoiding paying for professional legal services could be vastly outweighed by the costs that may result from your case not being appropriately handled. With rare exceptions, it is always beneficial to obtain some degree of legal advice before concluding your divorce.

Your choice of representation is not the only factor that will affect the cost of your divorce. The number and type of disagreements you may have with your spouse over the terms of your divorce will also determine the amount of work required to resolve the matter. Generally speaking, the longer a case takes and the more work a case requires, the more expensive it is. This is largely due to the fact that lengthy, contested cases result in more legal fees and costs. (Legal fees and costs are discussed in detail in Chapter 2 on page 17.) The manner in which a case proceeds naturally affects how expensive it ends up being to a client. Understandably, cases in which agreements are reached between the opposing lawyers are typically much less expensive than cases that go to court.

Simply put, the cost of legal representation is not insignificant, but you do have options, which will be discussed later in this book. In some cases, the costs associated with getting a divorce may limit a person's choice of attorney or the amount of assistance obtained. In others, it may not. It is important to have a general idea of what your divorce may cost so that you can adjust your divorce plan accordingly and make informed decisions regarding legal representation. The information in the next chapter will prepare you to ask the right questions when meeting with prospective attorneys and help you to determine the best path to take in your case.

CONCLUSION

Choosing a divorce attorney is rarely an easy or quick task. Although the divorce period is never an easy time, try to proceed through it slowly and carefully. Thoughtful consideration needs to be given when seeking attorney referrals, meeting with prospective attorneys, and deciding who might be a good fit for you. Now that you know how to find a good divorce attorney, you need to learn how to meet and interview prospective legal representation.

2.

Consulting an Attorney

The breakdown of a marriage often happens over many years. Whether it is something that you, your spouse, or both of you have considered, divorce is not typically a surprise. In such cases, there is more time to plan, and you may decide to consult an attorney before the process of getting a divorce begins, or perhaps even before a final decision has been made on whether or not to get a divorce. For some, however, the need to consult an attorney is more immediate. Perhaps they need to respond to divorce papers they have received. Maybe they have just become aware of infidelity in the marriage, or of secret withdrawals or dissipation of shared assets. Whatever the case may be, preparing for your divorce by first consulting an attorney can provide you with invaluable information.

Planning allows you to think things through so you can later discuss these difficult issues rationally and civilly. It can help you to avoid acting rashly and taking a misstep (or, at least, to limit the number of times you do so), which can happen at the outset of a divorce case, when emotions run high.

This chapter discusses the steps to take to find and consult an attorney or several attorneys. It reviews the initial questions you will need to ask, which concern price, procedure, and what you might expect as you begin the divorce process. Lastly, it explains the attorney fees and costs you might expect in connection with your divorce.

PLAINTIFF VERSUS DEFENDANT

Before we start, let's cover a question that is probably on your mind right now: How does being the *plaintiff* (the person who begins the legal action of divorce) in a divorce case differ from being the *defendant* (the person at whom the legal action of divorce is aimed)? More specifically, you probably want to know how being one or the other will look in the eyes of the court. Thankfully, the facts are clear on this subject. It makes no difference which party you are in the case, and you should not worry about the distinction. The court will not have any preconceived notions about you as a plaintiff or defendant. Plaintiffs may not necessarily want to abandon their marriages, just as defendants may not have done anything in particular to cause their spouses to file for divorce. Each case comes with its own set of facts, and judges are well aware of this.

BEGINNING THE PROCESS

Once you have the names and contact information of a number of divorce attorneys, you can begin the process of hiring a divorce lawyer by calling or emailing their offices and making appointments. The initial meeting with an attorney is often referred to as an *initial consultation*. Some attorneys charge a flat fee for this consultation, while some do not. If an attorney's office does not mention there being a consultation fee at the time of your call, ask if there is one. Of course, ask how much the fee is if the answer is yes.

These meetings normally last about an hour. They are usually done in person but may be held virtually. It is likely that the attorney will not be able to gather enough information from an initial consultation to tell you the likelihood of your obtaining a certain result. More information than can be given during an initial consultation will be needed before such questions may be answered with any degree of certainty. The attorney should, however, be able to provide you with some general legal guidelines to help you to understand your position and dispel any unnecessary concerns. Many people come to these initial meetings having heard inaccurate information about the divorce process that has caused them to worry for no reason. In such cases, getting basic information from a reliable source is not only useful but also comforting.

Filling Out Consultation Paperwork

You will normally be asked to sign paperwork from the attorney's office that confirms your consultation and related fee, if any. It will likely include language that states you have not yet hired the attorney

CONSULTING AN ATTORNEY

for anything other than the consultation, and that the attorney does not yet represent you in your legal matter. Both you and the attorney will decide on the level of involvement the attorney will have, if any, in your legal matter following the consultation. You have to want to hire the attorney, and the attorney has to agree to represent you. If both you and the attorney decide to work together, the attorney will draft a representation agreement, which outlines the terms of representation and will require your review. If you consent to the terms of the agreement, you will then need to sign the document to hire the attorney officially.

Explaining the Problem

Prior to your consultation, you may also be asked to complete other paperwork, which may include questions about yourself, your marriage, or your impending divorce. This information will be used to assist the attorney in the initial consultation. The attorney will normally begin by asking you a little bit about yourself, and whether you are there to start the divorce process, respond to divorce paperwork you have been given, or simply learn more about the divorce process at this time in order to decide whether or not to go through with it.

The questions will usually turn to the status of your marriage. The attorney will likely want to know how long you have been married, where you and your spouse live, if you have any children, and the work and health statuses of both you and your spouse. You will then be asked about the breakdown of your marriage and reasoning behind getting a divorce. This is your opportunity to tell your story and you should be as prepared as possible to do so. Jot down a few notes before your meeting and use them for reference if necessary. It can be very helpful to present your history in chronological order, although it is common to start with information you consider most important or concerning.

Most attorneys have lots of experience receiving and organizing information. They are also good at gathering information, so don't worry if you think you are not able to "get it all out." Some people are comfortable and quite capable of providing all the necessary information, some are not. That's okay. Most attorneys will realize that you are probably dealing with a lot of emotions at this time, and a good attorney will help you get through the consultation successfully.

Asking Questions

At some point, the attorney will ask if you have any specific questions. The following is a list of questions to consider before your meeting. You may want to write them down and bring the list with you to your consultation. A knowledgeable attorney may provide you with answers to many of these questions before you even have a chance to ask them, but it will be nice to have the list to ensure that the questions most important to you are covered in the time allotted for the consultation. It is perfectly acceptable to bring along your notes and take notes during your consultation. Attorney consultations not only help you to decide who to hire but also prepare you for the realities of divorce that may lie ahead.

How Does the Process Begin?

You many wonder what paperwork needs to be filed, or how to respond if you've just received paperwork. Will you have to appear in court? What information may you need to gather?

What Is the Process Like?

It's natural to want to know what to expect after your divorce case has received an initial response or been filed. What steps will have to be taken? How long does each step typically take? Will you have to go to court? Will your spouse's attorney question you? How long will it take for your divorce to be finalized?

As My Attorney, What Will You Do on My Behalf?

Although you may have an idea of what an attorney is supposed to do for you, you would likely benefit from having the role of a divorce attorney explained in detail to you. What will the week-to-week and month-to-month work look like? How involved will you be in the process? How will you be kept informed of the events related to your case? How will decisions be made? How will your divorce attorney prepare you for court if necessary?

What Will Be Required of Me?

You will probably not be surprised to know that you will be responsible for assisting your attorney in your case. Your attorney may need your help with things like providing information, decision making, and gathering documents.

Based on My Case, What Documents or Other Information Should I Be Prepared to Provide?

You will need to provide your divorce attorney with any information deemed relevant to your case, which may include personal documents, financial records, names of potential witnesses, or photographs. An experienced attorney should be able to identify the types of information that will likely be required in your situation so you can start to address these items sooner rather than later.

How Much Control Will I Have?

It is important to know which decisions you will make and which decisions your attorney will make in relation to your divorce. This is your opportunity to discuss how much input you would like to have in your case, and to find out how the attorney will welcome your input.

Based on the Information I've Provided, What Can I Expect Going Forward?

As recently noted, it is highly unlikely that the attorney you consult will have enough information at the outset to predict any particular result or have a strong opinion on the likely outcome of your divorce. The attorney should, however, be able to gather enough information from your meeting to let you know what factors might work in your favor or be of concern as they relate to the law regarding a particular issue. The attorney should also be able to tell you, in general terms, how a court is likely to receive certain claims based on the limited facts of your case as known at that time.

What Obstacles Should I Be Prepared for?

While more information will be needed, an experienced attorney should be able to identify what an opposing attorney (the attorney who represents your spouse) may claim or use against you in your divorce matter, and let you know what actions you might be able to take now to address or at least prepare for these issues.

What Is Your Fee?

Will the fee to represent you be based on an hourly rate or fixed? If it is based on an hourly rate, what is this rate, and does it vary in relation to the different employees of the attorney's office who may also work on your case? Will a retainer be required? If so, what amount will be required as a retainer? "(For a full explanation of attorney fees and costs, see "Attorney Fees" below.)

Will There Be Other Costs in Addition to Attorney Fees?

What additional costs might be expected in your case, and how are these costs typically paid? Have billing explained to you in detail.

Is There Anything I Can Do to Keep Costs Down?

The attorney you consult should be able to give you some advice on how to keep your divorce-related expenses down, so don't be shy to bring up the subject. (For tips on how you might be able to keep your costs down in this matter, see "Ten Ways to Save Money on Attorney Fees" on page 26.)

A competent attorney should be able to answer any of these questions with ease. Due to time limitations, however, you may have to schedule a follow-up consultation to address all your concerns. The scheduling and cost of this additional consultation should be discussed with the attorney prior to leaving the initial consultation.

ATTORNEY FEES

Divorce attorneys may charge for their services in a number of different ways. It is important that you understand the different types of billing so you can make an informed decision and plan for such expenses.

Retainer

Most attorneys who practice family law charge by the hour and require a retainer to take on a new client. A *retainer* refers to a certain amount of money paid in advance, which the attorney places in a trust account. This money will be used to pay for the hours billed in the future. As work is performed and fees are charged, funds from the retainer are moved from the trust account to the firm's account. In addition to your attorney's hourly fee, any expenses incurred by your attorney in your case, such as marshal fees or court fees, will typically be reimbursed to the law firm via the retainer. And what are these fees? *Marshal fees* may be incurred for paperwork that must be served to another person, and *court fees* may include amounts charged for filing or obtaining paperwork.

The individual attorney, or the attorney's firm, will determine the amount required as a retainer—in other words, how much money you will have to deposit in the trust account. This amount will be based partly on the attorney's hourly rate and partly on the expected complexity of your case. Generally, the more complicated the case, the higher the retainer. This is understandable because a complex case will require more of the attorney's time. Complex cases often involve more paperwork to obtain and review, more court proceedings to prepare for and appear at, and longer negotiations.

For instance, a case that is expected to proceed amicably is going to require a smaller retainer than a case that involves disputed financial issues. Similarly, a case that involves deciding where a child is going to live will likely require a higher retainer than one that deals merely with financial matters. Of course, different attorneys may have different opinions on how much time a prospective case will take, as well as differing hourly rates, so quotes for a retainer may vary from one attorney to another. Regardless, the retainer is often expected to be paid in full once the attorney has been officially hired. This detail may be negotiable if it's not possible for you to come up with the full retainer immediately. Many attorneys are more than willing to work out a payment plan if needed.

In addition, it is important to know what will happen to your retainer if it has not been completely depleted by the end of your case. This scenario may occur if your attorney finishes all work necessary or stops representing you for one reason or another. Will any of the unused funds be refunded? Some attorneys designate the retainer, or a portion of it, as a minimum payment, meaning you may receive some of your money back or possibly none at all. Other attorneys return all funds that have not been used in connection with their hourly billing.

If billing for the work done on your case exceeds your retainer, you may be expected to deposit another retainer at that time, although the amount of this retainer may differ from the amount of the initial deposit. If you are not asked for another retainer, you will still be responsible for any outstanding costs in connection with with billing or other fees after your initial deposit has been exhausted, assuming you are not being billed on a flat fee basis.

Any payment arrangements offered by an attorney should be part of your consideration when deciding on representation. Read and understand the terms of the fee agreement you sign so there are no surprises, and do not be afraid to ask questions.

Hourly Rate

As mentioned, most divorce attorneys charge an *hourly rate.* This means you are expected to pay a certain agreed-upon amount for the time your attorney spends on your case. More specifically, you are expected to pay a set amount for each hour of work done by your attorney. This hourly rate also applies to fractions of an hour worked. In other words, if your lawyer works on your case for half an hour, you would be charged half the hourly rate. If your lawyer works on your case for fifteen minutes, you would be charged a quarter of the hourly rate, and so on.

Keep in mind that most, if not all, law firms charge different hourly rates for different professionals within their firms. Paralegals will certainly be billed out at a lower rate than attorneys. Some administrative staff such as legal assistants may be billed out at lower hourly rates than paralegals. Other lawyers within the same firm may be billed out at different rates depending on their levels of experience or duties. You should be told and understand the different hourly rates at a firm and be assured that work on your case will be delegated in a cost-efficient manner. You may be able to reduce your bill by having certain questions or work directed to a lower-paid member of the firm. (For more ways to save on divorce-related expenses, see "Ten Ways to Save Money on Attorney Fees" on page 26.) Do not interpret this idea, however, as an invitation to try to micromanage your legal counsel. In the end, your attorney will be the person best qualified to determine which jobs should be delegated to which staff members in your case. It is important to understand your attorney's billing rates and fees, but unless something is truly concerning, you should trust that your attorney knows how best to structure your costs.

Attorneys and staff are obligated to keep track of all time spent on cases accurately and bill for their services accordingly. Customarily, itemized invoices are generated once a month so that clients can see what work was done, by whom it was done, how long it took, and what was charged for it. Review your bills. Attorneys and staff are not infallible, and good attorneys and firms will welcome any reasonable questions and fix any billing errors immediately.

Flat Fee

A *flat fee* arrangement means that an attorney will represent a client for a fixed sum instead of billing for services at an hourly rate. In other words, the client pays a set amount for the entire case, regardless of how much work or time the matter takes the attorney to complete. The flat fee may include the additional costs of the court and other providers, but will more than likely be limited to the attorney's fee. A fixed fee may be attractive to some clients, as it eliminates the uncertainty associated with the legal expenses of a case. Flat fees, however, are not commonly used in family law.

It can be difficult even for an experienced attorney to estimate accurately the total time a particular case will take, not yet being aware of the claims, arguments, or motivations of the client, let alone those of the client's spouse. In addition, attorneys often do not know who the opposing attorneys in divorce cases might be. Some opposing attorneys are easy to work with, while others are not. (An attorney who does not try to work things out prior to going to court and requires that all issues go to court is going to drive up costs because more time will be required to move the case to resolution.) Finally, attorneys may be unsure of the level of assistance they might receive from the court. Some judges and court personnel are very proactive in moving cases along and helping parties reach an agreement, while others are not so proactive or helpful. Cases in which the latter applies tend to last longer.

Since neither you nor your attorney will know with certainty how long your case will take or how much work will be involved, you will both be taking a bit of a risk with a flat fee. If your case turns out to be easy and quick, your flat fee may end up being higher than the hourly billing amount would have been. If your case turns out to be difficult and lengthy, your flat fee may end up being lower than the hourly billing amount you would have been charged.

Ten Ways to Save Money on Attorney Fees

Legal fees are expensive, but legal advice is invaluable when you are facing a legal issue. In light of this fact, it's good to apply a few strategies that can help you to balance the need for representation with the need to keep as much money in your wallet as possible.

1. **Consolidate Calls and Emails.** Unless time is of the essence, hold off on the urge to call, email, or text your attorney for each question or concern that pops up. It is generally better and more cost-efficient to take note of your questions and then ask them all in one call or email (not a long text).

2. **Organize Your Production.** Your attorney is most likely going to request that you provide lots of requested information. It takes a lot less time for an attorney to review information that has been placed in chronological order in advance and includes notes that explain each item.

3. **Start at the Bottom of the Pay Scale.** When you pay by the hour, there are usually different hourly rates for different professionals at a firm. Instead of contacting your attorney for all concerns, consider contacting someone else in the firm who charges a lower hourly rate first. Most reputable attorneys have paralegals or legal assistants that assist with each case who may be able to answer certain questions.

4. **Take Notes or Bring a Friend.** When you meet with your attorney, it is likely that you will be given a lot of information on legal and procedural issues. It is also likely that you will be in an emotionally difficult state. This combination often results in clients having a limited ability to retain all that is discussed during a meeting. Taking notes or having a second pair of ears with you will help you to keep everything straight and reduce the need to follow-up with the attorney to reiterate the topics discussed. Ask your attorney, however, before bringing someone else to a meeting. Some may object or will want to discuss any attorney-client privilege implications beforehand.

5. **Arrive Prepared.** Whether you are going to a meeting or a deposition, or to court, be sure to bring all the information requested of you. Often these events have to be rescheduled because required information is not available, which delays the process unnecessarily and increases costs. Contact your attorney's office prior to a scheduled event to confirm what items, if any, you are supposed to bring with you.

6. **Act in a Timely Manner.** Whatever you are supposed to do by court order, agreement, or on your attorney's advice, be sure to do it by the time ordered, stated, or requested. Being tardy will result in unnecessary motions being filed against you, as well as letters and phone calls to your attorney that require responses, resulting in more billable hours.

7. **Accept Reasonable Explanations from Your Attorney.** You should always understand and be kept informed of where your case is, how it got there, and where it is heading. You should be counseled on the basic legal principles that apply to your matter, how the law applies to the facts of your case, what obstacles may be presented by the opposing party, and your chances of obtaining a favorable result. It's not necessary or cost-efficient, however, for you to insist upon receiving a complete analysis of the law, every conceivable option that exists for the application of the law, every conceivable response the opposing side or the judge may have, etc.

8. **Let Your Attorney Represent You.** It's true that you and your attorney are a team. Every team has a captain. Let your attorney be the captain. Trust in your attorney's experience and expertise, which is easy to do when you feel confident that your attorney is acting in your best interests, with empathy and enthusiasm. Remember, these were the qualities you looked for when choosing an attorney.

9. **Tell Your Attorney Everything Up Front.** Trial attorneys start to build their cases from initial meetings with clients. Sometimes clients leave out vital information due to embarrassment,

oversight, or selective memory. If previously undisclosed information comes out later in a client's case, it may require the client's attorney to approach the case differently. For an attorney, this can be like trying to add an extra egg to a cake that's already baking in the oven. Don't risk jeopardizing your case by leaving things out.

10. **Pay for a Consultation.** Consulting an attorney prior to retaining the attorney's services can be very beneficial. An attorney can review your case, discuss options, and answer questions—all of which can help you to decide if and how to proceed. A consultation can also be helpful to those who must represent themselves due to financial reasons.

Apart from these tips, if you have limited funds available for legal representation, you may be able to obtain partial representation. (See page 14.) This option may be explored and explained during a consultation.

Hybrid Fee Structure

Sometimes an attorney will offer a hybrid fee structure to minimize the risk of overpayment or underpayment of legal fees. In this case, usually the client and attorney agree to a flat fee to cover work up to a certain point, usually prior to any trial preparation. If the case concludes prior to trial preparation, usually nothing more is owed. If the case does not conclude before trial preparation, and if a trial is necessary, then the work done in connection with both trial preparation and the trial itself will be billed at an hourly rate that has already been agreed upon by both the attorney and the client.

In a hybrid payment plan, you will likely have to provide a retainer at the time the hourly rate starts. The amount of the retainer may be agreed upon beforehand as well, allowing you to prepare for the possible cost ahead of time.

Caution

Be wary of attorneys who ask for very small retainers or no retainers at all, or who quote fees that are much lower than average for your area. It bears reminding that if something sounds too good to be true, it usually is. Attorneys who draw clients in with low rates or retainers usually provide lackluster service or surprise clients with big bills later on. Always check out online reviews from former clients of the attorneys you are considering for your case, which can be very helpful in the selection process.

Costs beyond Attorney Fees

You should expect to encounter other divorce-related expenses other than attorney fees. These other costs may include payments to other people or entities that are a customary part of the divorce process. For example, the court will charge a fee for opening your case. If you require a marshal to serve any paperwork, there will be a fee for this service, payable directly to the marshal. If a house or some other asset needs to be appraised, an appraiser will charge a fee for this service. Charges for transcripts of court proceedings are not uncommon. Such records are crucial when one needs to have proof of what was said in court or during a deposition (a proceeding in which one party is questioned under oath by the opposing attorney for the purpose of obtaining information relevant to the case). Sometimes the services of private investigators or financial auditors are necessary, resulting in additional costs.

Some of these additional expenses are related to mandatory services, but most are associated with optional ones. Your attorney should explain all expected and recommended services. For those that are not mandatory, your attorney should discuss with you the benefits and costs of each proposed service so you can decide if it is something you wish to use (and pay for).

In many instances, with your knowledge and consent, your attorney will use some of your retainer to pay court fees and other administrative fees. In some cases, with your permission, your attorney may pay these expenses on your behalf and then bill you for reimbursement. Otherwise, you will be expected to pay for these services directly. While attorney fees vary, other divorce-related fees, including court costs, should be the same regardless of the attorney you choose to represent you. All expected fees should be discussed during the interview process so you don't run into any surprises down the road.

Final Tip

All representation agreements between you and your attorney should be in writing and contain all the terms discussed. Itemized bills should be provided on a regular schedule. The more forthright and honest you and your attorney are with each other about fees, costs, and expectations, the more comfortable you will be discussing these issues—and the representation in general—over the course of your divorce case.

CONCLUSION

You may meet with one attorney and decide this person is the attorney for you. You may find it necessary, however, to meet with several attorneys before you find the right person. You will likely find that different attorneys have different styles of representation, and different ideas about how to handle your case. Don't be surprised if this happens. The law is more of an art than a science. In family law, there are very few strict formulas or rules. Instead, there are many factors that are taken into consideration by the court, with subjective weight given to each factor. A judge may consider a case quickly or at length to arrive at a result that is "fair" or "in the best interests of the children." Judges may also have different opinions on what information they find credible and relevant. This means there may be a number of ways for an attorney to approach an issue or achieve a desired result.

The initial consultation is the first step in your divorce. And as the saying goes, the hardest part of any journey is the first step. It solidifies your intention and direction, although there is no shame in changing direction or even backtracking when necessary. Getting the correct information and guidance early on will increase your chances of traveling on a straight path and having a smoother ride. In other words, you are off to a good start. You are now armed with lots of valuable information and will likely choose the right attorney for your case.

The next chapter covers important additional information you can obtain from your attorney that will likely be useful to you at the outset of your divorce. If time allows, you may address some of these issues with the attorneys you contact before hiring representation, although you may prefer simply to wait and get the advice of the attorney you hire to represent you.

3.

Preparation

At the start of a divorce, there are a number of practical tips that can help you to take appropriate action in your case when necessary. These tips address matters of concern such as automatic orders, documentation, passwords and electronic information, new email addresses, new mailing addresses, medical care, financial concerns, evidence, and long-term planning. As explained in the previous chapter, you may be able to obtain some of this important additional information regarding the divorce process from your attorney in the early stages of your divorce, or even from one or more of the attorneys you interview before hiring representation.

While all the following subjects are important to be aware of in a divorce, keep in mind that not all divorce cases unfold in the same way. Some are very challenging and contain a good deal of distrust between the parties, whether this distrust is warranted or not. Some cases proceed smoothly and amicably. Not all the following topics and suggestions will necessarily apply to your case. Your attorney will help you to determine what is relevant to your circumstances.

AUTOMATIC ORDERS

Prior to or at the beginning of a divorce, spouses may make bad or questionable decisions—sometimes in anger or spite, and sometimes in an attempt at self-protection. It may be very tempting to lock a spouse out of the home, remove a spouse from medical insurance coverage or an automobile insurance policy, hide money or other valuable assets from a spouse, or move children out of state, but these actions can lead to devastating and far-reaching consequences—consequences that may not be fully appreciated by the spouse making the decision.

In an effort to protect spouses and children from becoming victims of poor behavior during a divorce, sometimes a court creates *automatic orders*, which apply to both spouses at the start of a divorce and are listed on a court form. The plaintiff's attorney attaches this form to the initial divorce paperwork. This document specifically addresses the possibility of spiteful behavior during the divorce, such as the actions recently described, and is meant to minimize damage and unnecessary litigation. Automatic orders are wide-ranging and designed to prevent both spouses from behaving badly during the period of divorce. They are also aimed at keeping a couple's current finances and living circumstances in place until further orders of the court are issued.

Automatic orders apply to the plaintiff upon this party's signing of the initial paperwork to begin a divorce, and to the defendant upon this party's being properly served the divorce paperwork. If a party in a divorce violates any of these orders, the court may make a finding of contempt, which could result in the offending party's being penalized financially or even imprisoned. In addition, a violation of these orders could negatively affect the outcome of the offending party's case. While these orders and the possible consequences of not adhering to them do not guarantee good behavior, they have more than likely kept many people from going astray. Keep in mind that automatic orders do not address or affect any bad actions a spouse may have undertaken before they went into effect. If necessary, however, these actions can still be addressed and rectified by the court moving forward.

If you are the plaintiff in a divorce case, it is important to be aware of these orders and review them prior to starting your divorce action. If you have been served divorce paperwork and are now the defendant in a case, it is also vital that you be aware of these orders and fully understand them. If you have any questions or concerns regarding these orders, make sure to discuss them with your attorney.

DOCUMENTATION

As discussed in detail in Chapter 4, you will be required to provide your attorney with a lot of information during the divorce process. This information usually takes the form of paperwork that you will either create or obtain. Much of it will be financial in nature and relate to your spouse's and your income, assets, debts, and expenses. If you

PREPARATION

are someone who knows very little about your household income, assets, or bills, and are worried that your spouse is going to try to hide or change information relating to these matters once the divorce process begins, voice this concern to your attorney. In such a case, it would likely be in your best interests to try to obtain copies of all relevant financial records prior to the start of the divorce—or as early as possible if the divorce has already started—provided it would be safe to do so. These records may include income tax returns, bank account statements, investment account statements, and retirement account statements of both parties. (For more information on the items that are commonly required at the start of a divorce, see Chapter 4 on page 43.)

The process of searching for and making copies of these records should take place while your spouse is not present if you'd rather not have your actions be known to your spouse. Actual paper copies of these documents are best, but if it is not possible for you to make paper copies, simply take pictures of these items. Just make sure that all the information on the documents may be easily read in the photographs you take. If you have access to a scanner, you may also scan them and save them digitally. Copies of these documents should be kept in a safe place outside the marital home. Ideally, they should be given to your attorney. Unless your attorney states otherwise, you do not need to possess the originals for your case.

SPECIAL PROPERTY

If you are about to file for divorce or suspect your spouse may be about to do so, you may be worried about sentimental or irreplaceable items of yours disappearing or being damaged during the divorce period. If so, discuss the removal of these items from the home with an attorney before the process of divorce begins to unfold. If you are the plaintiff, this would mean removing the items prior to your attorney signing the paperwork that initiates the divorce action, known as the *summons and complaint*. If you are the defendant, this would mean removing the items prior to your being served with the initial divorce paperwork. The spouse who initiates the divorce will likely be at an advantage when it comes to this issue, but more often than not the other spouse is aware that paperwork is on the way.

Your heirlooms, family photos, scrapbooks, jewelry, journals, diaries, passport, and computer backup drives are all examples of property that may fall into the category of "special." Don't sell or destroy any of these items. Put them in a safe place. Document them with pictures and make a comprehensive list of the items. Be prepared to provide the list and pictures to both your attorney and your spouse or spouse's attorney for full disclosure. Regardless of whether or not you are the plaintiff or defendant, if your divorce has already started, you will likely have to notify and seek agreement from your spouse before removing any property. Your attorney will advise you.

The contents of any safes or safe deposit boxes should be documented in case these items end up disappearing. Cash is something that frequently goes missing from safes, and it is difficult to prove who took it, even with documentation.

PHOTOGRAPHS

Take photos of every room in the house—especially if you are planning to move out—to document the decor and show the condition of the entire house. Be sure to include items of particular value, such as art or antique furniture. Sometimes one spouse will cause damage to the house or its furnishings—especially if this spouse thinks the other will acquire the house in the divorce or receive the proceeds of its sale—and blame the other for it or say the damage happened years ago. There have been cases in which spouses have punched holes in walls, caused water damage on wood floors or furnishings, removed doorknobs, or worse.

PASSWORDS AND ELECTRONIC INFORMATION

Change all your passwords for your social media, email, and banking accounts, and for any other sensitive electronic information. In addition, be sure to create backups of all your computer files in case your computer disappears or your information is deleted. Copies can be stored on an external hard drive, your smart phone, or the cloud. If you don't know how to create backup copies of your files, ask someone who does to help you or seek professional assistance. And remember not to delete anything.

NEW EMAIL ADDRESS

Establish a new email account and dedicate it solely to your legal correspondence. Many people want to use their work email addresses, but these are not private. Either by law or by contract, most, if not all, employers have the right to access work emails. These emails are often stored on the employer's computer server and can be retrieved in the future.

NEW MAILING ADDRESS

Rent a PO Box and redirect all your individual mail there. Some people who are going through a divorce are faced with having their mail taken and sometimes read by their spouses, which may include divorce-related legal correspondence or even bills that, as a result, go unpaid. If you think this scenario may apply in your case, consider having your mail redirected. For bills in your name, you should be able to switch from being sent physical invoices to receiving electronic ones, known as "paperless billing," which you should direct to your new email address.

MEDICAL CARE

If you are on your spouse's health insurance, consider obtaining any necessary medical treatment now, especially if the coverage is good or likely better than what you will be able to get for yourself following your divorce. Furthermore, any out-of-pocket costs you incur from these treatments will likely be considered joint debt, so these expenses may be divided between you and your spouse instead of being yours alone following your divorce.

If you will need to acquire health insurance coverage following your divorce, your attorney may be able to refer you to someone who can review coverage options and costs with you. It is likely that this person will need to know what your income will be at the time you apply for coverage. Unfortunately, it may be difficult for you to estimate your future income in light of divorce-related matters such as child support and spousal support, which may impact your income after your divorce, whether you receive these payments or have to pay them. Nevertheless, it is never too early to identify someone to work with and start getting some basic information about coverage options and costs.

FINANCIAL CONCERNS

The following issues come up frequently enough at the start of a divorce to warrant special consideration. They involve the temptation to hide assets from a spouse, the uncertainty regarding accessing joint funds, and the funding options available for legal fees and living expenses as the divorce process begins.

Hiding Assets

Some people may feel the need to protect their money or property from their spouses. They may want to know if they can transfer certain assets to another individual or otherwise hide them in some way. This is a big no-no. An attorney cannot legally advise you on how to hide your assets, and if you pursue this action and get caught, you could be charged with perjury or fraud, and it most certainly will negatively affect the outcome of your case. In addition, the attorney who aided and abetted you in this action would likely face sanctions.

You are required to disclose all your financial information fully and accurately during the divorce process, including all income, expenses, assets, and debts, and it is very difficult to eliminate all traces of valuable assets. A vigilant opposing attorney will almost always be able to spot red flags that indicate missing assets. If your spouse's lawyer can't find them, a forensic accountant (see the inset on page 38) may be brought in to help in the matter. Once you've been caught, your credibility will be shot, making the rest of your case an uphill battle.

Despite an attorney's best efforts to develop supporting evidence in a case, most divorce cases come down to the testimonies of the two parties involved. If it is shown that you have lied, tried to deceive, or otherwise acted in bad faith in regard to your finances during the divorce process, this knowledge will cast doubt on all other statements you've made and will make. From then on, you will likely come out on the losing side of any judgment concerning conflicting testimony.

In addition, the court may hold your bad actions against you when handing down any temporary or final divorce orders. It is a much better use of your time and money to identify and develop a basis for your claims in order to reach the best possible outcome in your divorce case. This is true for all divorce-related issues, but warrants highlighting here, as the temptation to do something secretive with finances is often quite strong in the initial stages of a divorce, when emotions tend to run high.

Joint Accounts

If you have joint bank accounts with your spouse and are worried money might disappear once a divorce has been filed, it may be acceptable to withdraw or transfer up to half the amount of available funds in these accounts to a bank account that is solely in your name. This possibility should be discussed with your attorney to determine whether it would be advisable for you to pursue and would not negatively impact your case. Technically, most banking rules allow either spouse to withdraw all funds from a joint account, but doing so never looks good to a judge and usually causes problems down the road.

If you think taking half or any of the available funds in your joint accounts will cause your spouse to become violent, then perhaps it is not the best thing to do on your own. Instead, ask your attorney how you may be able to obtain this money through a temporary court order. Regardless, it's important to keep copies of all applicable bank statements and create a paper trail of any funds taken. Until your divorce is final and the division of your finances and assets is complete, use these funds only for necessary or customary living or household expenses, business expenses, or attorney fees related to your divorce. Again, have your attorney review legally acceptable expenditures with you.

Accessing Funds for Attorney Fees and Other Expenses

Depending on your situation, you may be in need of additional funds for living expenses either now or immediately after your divorce proceedings begin. In all likelihood, you will need to pay an attorney in advance to start work on your case. If you do not have any funds or not enough funds in your name alone, and you have no joint bank accounts with your spouse that you can access safely, then a credit card could be used to pay attorney fees and as a source of cash.

If you have sole control of your credit card account, it might be better to charge what you need for your initial attorney fees and living expenses until you can obtain some other form of temporary support. If your credit card lists your spouse as the primary account holder, however, you may only have a small window of time in which to obtain a cash advance or make a charge to retain an attorney before you are removed as an authorized user.

If you have access to other liquid assets, such as mutual funds or stocks, you may have the ability to convert these into cash to obtain funds for necessary living expenses and attorney fees. Again, consult your attorney on this matter and keep excellent financial records, as you will eventually need to account for any liquidated funds.

Retirement accounts should be the last accounts to consider liquidating. Besides the need to keep these funds in place for the future, there is a greater chance that taxes and penalty fees for withdrawing these funds early will be high. You should consult a tax professional (someone who is not going to report your actions or decisions to your spouse) to determine which accounts, if liquidated, would produce the least financial harm to your short- and long-term situations.

If none of the previously described options are viable, then you may need to borrow funds. It is advisable to discuss this issue with your prospective attorney and try to determine what a realistic retainer is going to cost. If the person from whom you borrow money is able to lend you an amount that exceeds the cost of the retainer, try to calculate what you will need to cover your immediate financial requirements. It is in your best interests to be as honest and accurate as possible with whoever is willing to lend you money. It is usually best to put your loan in writing if you are expected to pay it back. It is also wise to discuss this issue with your attorney before borrowing any funds.

Forensic Accountants

If financial misappropriation or abuse (sometimes referred to as "financial infidelity") is a concern, then your attorney may recommend hiring a *forensic accountant*. These individuals are experts in finding and tracking financial transactions and analyzing how money is coming in and being used. They are financial detectives. The ability of a forensic accountant to assist you in your case will depend upon the information available, of course.

If necessary (and practical), your attorney can ask the court to order your spouse to provide you with funds at the beginning of your case or anytime your case is pending so you can return any funds you have borrowed. Upon request by either spouse, the court can also make financial orders for both parties to follow while the divorce is pending to ensure that each spouse has enough funds to pay attorney fees and cover living expenses. These financial orders may obligate one spouse to pay a certain amount of money to the other spouse on a weekly basis, pay the expenses of the other spouse directly, or transfer a lump sum to the other spouse or spouse's attorney.

EVIDENCE

Evidence is something that can be used by one spouse or the other to help either prove or disprove a claim. Evidence can come in many forms. Oral statements made under oath during a court proceeding are evidence. This type of evidence is referred to as *testimony*. Other types of evidence usually involve paperwork, which may include invoices, medical records, contracts, pay stubs, and tax returns. Printouts of electronic communications such as emails, social media posts, or texts may also be used as evidence. Non-textual evidence may include photographs, voice messages, and video recordings.

While your attorney will assist you in identifying and securing evidence during your case, you may find it beneficial to consult your lawyer on the evidence you may need to acquire before the divorce process starts or soon after it has begun.

SOCIAL MEDIA

Before the existence of social media, it could be rather difficult to gather evidence of a spouse's infidelity, second job, undisclosed travel, hidden property, ability to work, extra income, etc. Back then, clients would show up at their attorneys' offices with a few letters, cards, pictures, and maybe some financial documents, and sometimes a private investigator would be hired to get more substantial evidence. Private investigators may still be needed in certain cases, but thanks to social media, spouses and their attorneys have never had an easier time gathering evidence to support divorce-related claims on their own.

> ### Caution While Preparing For Your Divorce
>
> If you need to prepare for your divorce but are fearful that doing so might tip off your spouse to your intentions, consider paying for your attorney consultation fee in cash or have someone else pay it so the expense won't show up on your bank or credit card statement. In addition, be mindful that suspicious spouses may use tracking software on their partners' cell phones or hide tracking devices in their vehicles to monitor their whereabouts. If you think these circumstances could apply to you, you may also want to consider meeting your potential attorney at a location other than the attorney's office, if possible, or conducting a virtual meeting from a safe location, such as the home of a friend or family member.

Many people document their whole lives, in some form or another, online. It is now possible to know where some people are at any given time of day, who they are with, and what they are doing. You can determine what they bought, when they bought it, and for whom they bought it. You can often gain access to the people they associate with, and see what all these people are posting about—which may include their spouses. Social media has turned what were once private conversations into evidence.

With the advent of online payment platforms, the amount of available information has increased even more. It is not unusual for infidelity to be discovered simply because an individual made an online payment—using Venmo, Zelle, PayPal, etc.—to a family member who could then see that other payments had been made to a third party who ended up being an extramarital partner. People are simply not aware how traceable their transactions are, or it could be that they don't care. As a result, online searches are a good place to start when gathering information to support any claims you think you or your attorney may want or need to prove in your divorce case. And since online histories are often deleted (or made much more difficult to access) once a divorce has commenced, it is advisable to browse your spouse's online platforms and financial transaction history beforehand if you have the opportunity to do so.

PREPARATION

Some people start this process on their own, taking screenshots of anything they suspect may be relevant. Some people hire others to do the work for them. Your attorney may be able to refer you to the appropriate professionals who can help in such matters.

PRIVATE INVESTIGATOR

If you suspect your spouse of cheating or engaging in any kind of illicit activity, you will want to gather documented evidence of such behavior. As previously suggested, this task may require hiring a private investigator. It is best to consult your attorney about hiring a private investigator before filing for divorce, if possible. Your spouse will likely act more carefully or cease engaging in any questionable activity once the divorce process has started, so you should try to give the private investigator enough time to gather evidence before you file. If your divorce has already begun, you and your attorney can discuss whether you might still benefit from using the services of a private investigator.

When hiring a private investigator, you will need to discuss costs, which will likely include a separate retainer. You will also need to supply the private investigator with certain information, such as a picture of your spouse; the make, model, year, color, and license plate number of your spouse's car; where your spouse works; and a general outline of your spouse's comings and goings. Finally, you will need to explain what you believe your spouse is doing, and how you learned about these actions. Depending on the situation, the private investigator may require more information.

CONTACTS

Throughout the divorce process, there will be numerous people with whom you will need to get in touch. For this reason, you should keep a record of all of your professional providers. Write down the names and contact information of these individuals (insurance brokers, financial managers, CPAs, attorneys, therapists, etc.) and have this information at the ready. Chances are that your attorney will need it—if not right away, then eventually.

LONG-TERM PLANNING

With the help of your attorney, it may be advisable for you to explore what your living and work situations may look like following the divorce. Your divorce will necessarily lead to a change in your personal living arrangements. If you have children with your spouse, it will also lead to a change in your family's living arrangements, your family's expenses, and the amount of time you spend parenting.

Will you be able to continue working? Will you need to transition back into the workplace? Will you need to obtain any further education? Will childcare costs increase? How will additional expenses be handled? Could any debts be reduced prior to your divorce? Is it advisable to consider filing for bankruptcy prior to dissolving the marriage and possibly selling the marital home? Should any expenses be incurred prior to your divorce?

Addressing these "big picture" items will probably require additional consultations with your attorney, and possibly your meeting with an accountant or financial advisor. At the very least, it will involve quite a bit of thought, self-reflection, and investigation on your part. The work you put in now, however, will pay off later. The better prepared you are, the better you will be able to handle anything that comes your way.

CONCLUSION

By now you've got a lot to think about: How to find an attorney, what information to seek out, and how to start preparing for the divorce process to ensure the best outcome possible. Your work has only just begun. Your attorney is going to need a lot of information from you. The next chapter outlines what this information will likely entail so that you may start obtaining it.

4.

Discovery

Discovery is a term used to describe the process of gathering and exchanging information that may be presented during your case, which may include documents, pictures, recordings, or any other items that may pertain to your divorce. It is designed to prevent both parties in a case from being surprised by unexpected evidence. When both parties have access to the same information, each party can get a better sense of how the case should proceed.

Just about every legal dispute involves a certain amount of discovery. Attorneys use this information to establish facts, evaluate the strengths or weaknesses of a claim, and determine settlement options. Of course, it is also used as evidence when necessary. You and your spouse will have to assist your attorneys by providing them with a good deal of information, typically in the form of paperwork and by answering questions.

REQUESTS FOR DOCUMENTS

Discovery is an ongoing process that takes place throughout a divorce case. At the beginning of a case, each spouse's attorney will typically send a written request to the other spouse's attorney for a long list of financial items, otherwise known as a *request for production*. Documentation related to something other than finances may be requested as well. The recipient of a request for production is normally given a specific period of time in which to comply with this request. Your attorney will likely want to review, organize, and prepare this information before sending it to your spouse's attorney, so try to obtain it as soon as you can. You or your attorney may object to some of the information requested, and this objection should be discussed between the two of you. In a divorce, everything that ever happened during the marriage may be relevant to the case, and the breadth of information that may be requested is considerable. If appropriate, however, your attorney may file an objection to any request that seems unwarranted. If the opposing attorneys cannot solve this problem between themselves, then a judge will settle the issue. Regardless, you should strive to gather all information requested by your spouse's attorney, whether or not you plan on raising any objections, as soon as possible.

Financial Documentation

One of the first things your spouse's attorney will ask you to provide will probably be a record of all your financial accounts. You will most likely not have to provide documentation in connection with any account you hold jointly with your spouse, as presumably your spouse will have equal access to this information. You will be obliged to provide your spouse's attorney with all financial information that is solely in your name alone or shared with someone else other than your spouse. If you are not in possession of requested information but can get this information with greater ease than your spouse, you have an obligation to obtain it. (Suggestions regarding who may have certain information and how to obtain this information are provided below.) Your attorney can assist you in locating this information as well.

Sometimes people are asked to bring requested documents or other items with them to a court proceeding such as a deposition. (See page 49 for more information on depositions.) Again, it is good practice to get these items to your attorney for review prior to the date of the court proceeding.

The following financial documents are usually required during divorce litigation:

- **Federal and State Income Tax Returns and Supporting Documentation.** This paperwork can be obtained from your tax preparer or accountant.

- **Pay Stubs or Records of Automatic Bank Deposits.** Payroll information may be obtained from your employer or from bank records showing deposits that have been made.

- **Credit Report.** A credit report is a history of your debts and debt-related payments. It can be obtained from one of the major credit reporting companies, which include Experian, TransUnion, and Equifax.

- **Social Security Statement.** This statement is a history of your earnings and can be obtained from the United States Social Security Administration.
- **Bank Statements, Credit Card Statements, and Investment Statements.** These documents may be obtained directly from the associated financial companies or banks, or through your financial advisor or accountant.
- **Retirement Account Statements.** This information may be obtained from your employer or directly from the financial company that manages your retirement account.
- **Life Insurance Policies Covering You and Your Spouse.** Copies of these life insurance policies may be obtained from the financial companies that issued them. Only the owner of a policy can obtain a copy, so if the policy covering your life or your spouse's life is solely in your spouse's name, you will not be required to produce it. Your spouse will likely have to provide it.
- **Health Insurance Coverage Costs.** This information may also include costs associated with COBRA. Statements may be obtained from your employer or health benefit agent.
- **Business Ownership Documentation.** These documents may be obtained from the attorney that assisted with the formation of the business. If your legal interest in the business was obtained after the formation of the business, the attorney who prepared the associated legal documents may be able to assist you in obtaining copies of applicable records—that is, documentation explaining your ownership rights.
- **Trust Documentation.** This documentation may be applicable to you or your spouse. It may be obtained from the probate attorney who assisted you or your spouse with the preparation of these documents.
- **Last Will and Testament, and Documentation Related to Any Estate Currently in Probate.** These documents may be obtained from the probate attorney handling any such estate.

- **Homeowner's Insurance or Renter's Insurance Policy.** A copy of this policy may be obtained from your insurance agent or the financial company that issued it.

- **Mortgage Deed and Note to Any Real Estate Owned By You or Your Spouse.** Copies of these documents may be requested from your closing attorney or the town hall associated with the property's location.

- **Appraisal of Any Real Estate Owned by You or Your Spouse.** A copy of a real estate appraisal may be requested from the person who appraised the property or the closing real estate attorney involved.

- **Contract of Employment.** You may request a copy of this document from your employer.

- **Credit Applications.** Copies of your credit applications (e.g., personal loans, car loans, mortgages, credit cards, etc.) may be obtained from the lending institutions associated with these applications.

- **Documentation Supporting Your Monthly Living Expenses.** Such documentation may include mortgage statements, utility bills, and invoices for automobile loans and automobile insurance. You may already have paper copies of these monthly bills, but if you have paperless billing, then you will need to access your associated online accounts and print them.

- **Documentation Concerning Outstanding Debt.** This debt may include credit card debt, outstanding personal loans, and outstanding medical or tax bills. Documentation of each debt may be obtained from the company or organization associated with it.

- **A Financial Affidavit.** A financial affidavit is a sworn statement given by you that declares your income, expenses, assets, and liabilities. Your attorney can assist you in preparing this document and it may be referred to by a different name in your state. (See Chapter 7 on page 87 for more information.)

Your attorney can tell you how much information to obtain in each category. Some information may need to go back several years, while other information may be limited to a current date. As your case goes on, your spouse's attorney may make what is known as a *supplemental request*, asking you to update your information or produce additional items. Your attorney will likely request the same information from your spouse. It is an ongoing process, as finances change over time, new information becomes known, and the attorneys have to be sure they are working with current information. Being aware of this reality will hopefully reduce your frustration with this part of your case.

You should be prepared for your spouse to take longer than perhaps you feel is necessary to provide requested information, whether this is done on purpose or not. Some people have reasons for dragging their feet. Some people simply aren't organized or motivated to put time and energy into the task. Very often, attorneys will have to follow up and file motions to compel spouses to comply with discovery requests.

How You Can Help

You can help to reduce attorney fees by obtaining your information on your own and providing it in good order to your attorney. "In good order" means that all copies should be legible, all documents are complete (contain all pages), and all documents and copies have been placed in chronological order. Bonus points if you "tab" or use sticky notes to label and identify each item you are providing and include their dates. If you are providing documents in electronic format, you should label documents clearly, as well as all folders and files. Remember that label names which may be obvious to you may not be obvious to the attorney or paralegal reviewing your documents, so take the time to make sure the label you give each document or electronic file clearly reflects and identifies the item. Double bonus points if you order and number the documents in the same order that they were requested (attorneys usually give clients a written list of requested documents) and note on a cover sheet whether any items are missing and why. By following this advice you will save your attorney's office time—thus saving yourself money—and allow your case to proceed in a timely manner.

Although your attorney will be doing most of the requesting, reviewing, and analyzing of information from your spouse, you may be able to assist with this process. It is perfectly acceptable to ask to review the list of requests for financial information or written questions prior to their being issued or prior to a deposition of your spouse being taken. You may be able to suggest a request, question, or line of questioning that your attorney has overlooked. After all, you are more likely to know more about your marriage and your spouse than your attorney does.

Likewise, you may ask to review the material that has been provided to your attorney by your spouse. You can do this for purely personal reasons, or you may be able to assist your attorney by noting anything that looks unusual or surprising. Perhaps you can answer any questions your attorney may have.

This level of involvement is reasonable and prudent, and your attorney should welcome such assistance. Take a tip from a former client of mine, who said, "Whether it's paper or digital records, being able to find and produce requested items is vital. I was lucky to be organized prior to the divorce. Filing, labeling, and storing things accessibly is important. I had a combative ex whose lawyer demanded piles of paperwork from me. As annoying as it was, I was able to come up with everything."

Non-Financial Documentation

Discovery beyond financial documents is often necessary when there are disputes over custody or the post-divorce parenting plan for children, or in regard to which party was responsible for the breakdown of the marriage. Your attorney will likely discuss these issues with you thoroughly, and together you can identify what information may be necessary to help prove or disprove a claim. While financial records may be relevant to your case, production for these types of issues usually consists of emails, texts, other electronic communications, journals, pictures, videos, and social media posts. Medical or school records may also be requested. Your spouse's attorney may ask you to produce such information as well.

REQUESTS FOR TESTIMONY

Through the initial divorce proceedings, you, either as the plaintiff or the defendant, may be required to provide either written or oral statements regarding your marriage. You may be asked to answer a list of questions in written format, known as *interrogatories*. Interrogatories are common and will usually include specific questions related to your finances, your work history, your health, the reasons for the breakdown of your marriage, and, if applicable, your preferences for a post-divorce parenting plan. You may be asked to admit or deny the truth of a number of statements under oath. This set of statements is known as a *request for admission.* Requests for admission are not particularly common in divorce cases, and when they do come up, the statements they include are extremely case-specific. Statements may relate to cash earnings, spending, relationships, and a person's living situation, among other things. You must address these statements to the best of your ability and then sign the document under oath, thereby swearing to the truthfulness of your answers. You will normally have a certain period of time to respond. Keep in mind that your attorney will assist you with your responses well before the due date.

You may also be required to answer questions in person at what is referred to as a *deposition*. In this case, your spouse's attorney will contact your attorney prior to the proceeding to let you know well in advance where and when the deposition is to take place. Your spouse's attorney will also list any documents you will be required to bring with you. A deposition will usually take place at the office of the attorney who has requested it. There will be a person there, hired and paid for by your spouse's attorney, who is authorized to confirm your identity and take your oath that the information you give will be truthful. This individual, commonly referred to as a *court reporter,* is also responsible for recording all that is said at a deposition. After a deposition, a court reporter then prepares a written transcript of the deposition for future use by the attorneys on the case and, if necessary, the court.

During your deposition, your spouse's attorney will ask you questions on various topics relevant to your marriage and divorce, which you will likely have to answer. The process usually takes a few hours but has been known to extend over an entire workday. Your attorney, your spouse, your spouse's attorney, and the court reporter are usually the only people in the room with you. Depositions can be intrusive and stressful, so it is important that your attorney prepare you for this proceeding.

WHAT AMOUNT IS ENOUGH?

The amount and type of discovery you do will depend on the particular facts of your case, your attorney's strategy, and discussions between you and your attorney. Cost is an important factor for many clients. It will take your attorney time not only to request the information, but also to review, summarize, and analyze it. Your attorney may take your spouse's deposition, which will also involve preparing the questions.

You may wonder whether all this gathering of information has to be done. At the very least, it is important and necessary for your attorney to review some basic financial information. If you have a decent understanding of your family's finances and do not suspect your spouse of any "funny business," and the initial financial review done by your attorney does not produce any red flags, then discovery may end there. If your case doesn't meet the three previous conditions, then more substantial discovery may be necessary. When this is the case, the cost to resolve any concerns is justified. Naturally, you and your attorney should attempt to narrow the scope of your requests in order to keep the amount of time spent on discovery within reason.

You won't have too much input or control over the amount of discovery your spouse's attorney chooses to do. Although you may end up being frustrated by excessive requests, try not to spend too much time worrying about them. Just do your best to cooperate in a timely manner and follow your attorney's instructions in regard to compliance. If you don't understand why something is being asked, don't be afraid to speak to your attorney about it.

CONCLUSION

Do you remember having to study for an important test in school that you didn't want to take? You may have felt worried, stressed out, and a bit overwhelmed. Sometimes the discovery process can bring on the same exact feelings—and just as you would for a test, you have to be prepared for what lies ahead. The discovery process may be cumbersome and last longer than you expected, but it is an important part of the divorce process. If you are in a position to plan for it, you should make it a priority. Often it is the person who can prove or otherwise support claims or defenses with documents or other evidence that obtains a better settlement outcome or trial decision. With complete and correct information in hand, your attorney will be in a better position to negotiate and advocate on your behalf.

The next chapter reviews options for divorce other than traditional litigation. One of the benefits of choosing to avoid litigation is that your case will usually require less paperwork than would be necessary if you were to take it to court. After reading this chapter, this benefit alone should be a powerful motivator for you to explore these alternatives.

5.

Getting a Friendly Divorce

Most of this book focuses on traditional litigation, in which each spouse is represented by an attorney. In this type of divorce process, typically all communication goes through the attorneys, and both parties go through the discovery process, as discussed in the previous chapter. If an agreement cannot be reached—whether on temporary rules to follow while the divorce is pending or the final financial and parenting divorce orders—the parties must then go to court and have the matter decided on by a judge.

This process, by its very nature, is adversarial, and many cases do fit that description. I'm sure you have heard your share of stories about bad break-ups, messy divorces, and divorces that cost a fortune and end badly for all parties. Many of these cases are fueled by anger and resentment on the part of one or both spouses. Some spouses are more focused on fighting with each other or proving the other wrong than on resolving their differences. And for some, the protections offered by traditional litigation may be absolutely necessary. But this is not true for everyone. There are couples that view their divorce as a problem to be solved, not a war to be won.

These couples do not wish to dwell on the past. Instead, they want to plan for a smooth and fair transition into the future. They are able to be friendly with each other. They do not wish each other harm. And they prefer to make decisions regarding their children together, without involving the court. In addition, they do not wish to spend their life savings on attorney fees. It is important to understand that there are options for those couples who strive to reach a mutually agreeable solution to the dissolution of their marriage.

Uncontested divorces, or "friendly divorces," as I refer to them, are possible within our traditional legal system. Many spouses can and do go through the "adversarial" process of divorce amicably, working together to reach an agreement. It takes a sustained effort and the cooperation of everyone involved, but it can be done. Attorneys can assist their clients in achieving this goal by making recommendations and conducting themselves in such a way as to support an amicable divorce process. Remaining calm and being respectful towards the opposing party and attorney are two ways an attorney can be helpful. Putting in the time and effort to address issues to the satisfaction of both parties, allowing their clients to compromise, and steering their clients away from going to court unnecessarily are other ways attorneys can help to resolve a divorce case in a friendly manner.

In such cases, formal discovery of financial information is often reduced, with clients' informed consent, and the attorneys are able to start working right away on the terms of the agreement, which quite often have been discussed between the spouses prior to hiring counsel.

This chapter looks at two types of divorce outside traditional litigation: mediation and collaborative divorce.

MEDIATION

You and your spouse may prefer to work out your parental and financial challenges outside the traditional litigation process, but you both may need some guidance, if not full legal representation, to do so. You may both be seeking mutual assistance in dissolving your marriage. This is where mediation comes into play. *Mediation* is an alternative method of dispute resolution for settling divorce or other legal matters. It is an effective, and often successful, substitute for litigation. Instead of beginning your divorce by searching for an attorney to represent you against your spouse, you and your spouse begin by searching for a mediator who will assist both parties in the process.

The Mediation Process

In mediation, spouses are given an opportunity to discuss, negotiate, and craft an agreement concerning all the terms of their divorce. A neutral mediator, who is usually an attorney or mental health provider, is present during these discussions to help facilitate this process, which normally takes place over a number of meetings at the mediator's office or virtually. During this process, no attorneys who may be assisting either you or your spouse are present. It normally includes only you, your spouse, and the mediator. The mediator is responsible for:

- providing a safe and private place to hold these discussions;
- ensuring equal participation and civility between spouses;
- directing the discussions;
- making sure all relevant topics are covered;
- facilitating exchanges of any financial information or other documents between spouses as necessary;
- keeping everyone on track, and providing feedback and guidance to prevent deadlock;
- referring spouses to specialists or bringing specialists to a mediation session as needed; and
- educating both parties about the divorce process in general.

If one or both spouses have any immediate issues they would like to address, these are usually discussed first. Sometimes a spouse will want to talk about the breakdown of the marriage. The mediator (and spouse) should acknowledge this desire and allow some productive discussion on why the parties are divorcing. The focus in mediation, however, should be on the future lives of the spouses and what the best co-parenting strategy would be if children are involved. Perhaps there is an immediate parenting concern or financial issue that needs attention. The mediator will try to help the parties discuss and resolve these matters.

Assuming no immediate issues need to be addressed, the first meeting will normally consist of discussing the parties' thoughts on a parenting plan if they have any children. This issue is usually negotiated with the mediator's help until an agreement is reached before moving on to other subjects. The mediator will likely review the parties' finances next. It is during this phase that child support, alimony, and property and debt distributions are negotiated. If the parties have discussed these issues prior to starting mediation or are close to agreement on many issues, then perhaps they will only need two or three mediation sessions before the mediator can outline an agreement. If no discussions have taken place, or the parties are far apart or financial information needs to be gathered and reviewed by spouses, then many more sessions may be required before the parties are able reach an agreement.

It is important to understand that mediators are not judges or arbitrators; they are not there to pick sides, offer opinions as to who is right and who is wrong, or make decisions. They are there to guide you and your spouse through the process.

Keep in mind that just because you are choosing to go through mediation, does not mean you cannot retain your own attorney to assist you, but such assistance will take place in private, outside mediation. It is not mandatory for you to hire an attorney. A spouse may choose to hire an attorney at the start of mediation to have access to legal advice and feedback throughout the process. This type of representation is sometimes referred to as a "mediator coach." A spouse may choose to hire an attorney towards the end of mediation to draft or review the final agreement. This type of representation is often referred to as "review counsel." It really doesn't matter what term is used, as long as you and your attorney are clear on what the attorney is doing for you. At the onset of mediation, your mediator should tell both you and your spouse that the option of having a mediator coach or review counsel is available.

Once a full agreement has been reached, it will be formalized in writing. The rest of the documents required by the court will also be prepared. You and your spouse will review and sign all the documents. This paperwork will then be filed with the court. If you have come to an agreement on all aspects of your divorce, you may have the option of waiving a court appearance and requesting that the court accept your agreement "on the papers." Your mediator will let you know if this option is available in your state and in your case. If it is, and assuming all is in order and the court has no questions, a judge will usually review all paperwork submitted and grant the divorce according to the agreement provided within a short period of time. Your mediator or attorney will receive notice and inform you that your divorce has been finalized. If you must appear in person for your divorce, the review will take place in court before a judge, and your divorce will likely be granted at that time.

The Benefits of Mediation

You may feel that the friendly process of mediation would be better for your mental health than litigation. While divorce will still be stressful, and fear of the unknown still present, it may be comforting to know that both you and your spouse will be working towards a common goal of reaching an agreement that both parties will find acceptable. Benefits of mediation include the fact that you will not be ambushed by your spouse's attorney, a spotlight will not be cast on any of your less than stellar marital moments, and your divorce will not focus on the worst aspects of your marriage. If you have children with your spouse, mediation will also benefit their well-being during the divorce process. Mediation will also help to give the divorce process a measure of efficiency and provide both parties with privacy and control.

Efficiency

Successful mediation allows divorcing couples to avoid the delays and costs associated with traditional divorce litigation. First and foremost, it means you won't be at the mercy of the court's schedule. The wait to get a hearing date for disputed matters can be many months. Even then, your time with the judge can be continued to another day or shortened so much that your hearing cannot be completed in one day, particularly if too many matters have been scheduled for that day or there are not enough judges present. These scenarios are not uncommon.

While there is nothing preventing attorneys from discussing matters and moving a case forward while awaiting a hearing, it is often the case that nothing gets accomplished during this time. In contrast, if you and your spouse work with a mediator, you should be able to schedule meetings in a timely manner. By working cooperatively towards the same goal of reaching an agreement, you and your spouse will also be more likely to be punctual when it comes to fulfilling any requests and generally prepared to participate in the process.

Mediation is often less expensive than traditional litigation, as it is usually less time consuming and thus results in fewer hours being billed—even if you and your spouse each hire separate legal counsel as well. This outside legal assistance usually requires much less of an attorney's time than would traditional litigation. This attorney will not be negotiating your agreement or preparing you for court. Most of this individual's work will consist of answering your legal questions, advising you, preparing you for your mediation sessions, and reviewing documents—and all of these services are used only at your request, allowing you to control your costs to a certain degree.

Privacy

Mediation is conducted more privately than litigation, usually taking place at the mediator's office. In most instances, sessions are only attended by you, your spouse, and the mediator. Sessions are not recorded, and everything said during mediation is confidential—neither the mediator nor the spouses can be called to testify in connection with what was said during mediation. The purpose of this confidentiality is to encourage participants to be open and honest with each other during mediation and eliminate any possible fear that something they say may be used against them at a later date, such as an admission of infidelity, improper use of marital assets, or what kind of financial terms would be acceptable to avoid trial.

In contrast, court matters are public proceedings. Not only can any person attend and watch your hearing, but the proceedings are recorded and transcripts of your and your spouse's testimonies can be ordered by anyone. Depositions, common during the discovery process in traditional litigation, are also recorded and transcribed. Mediation discussions, however, are not a matter of public record that your children or others would be able to see.

Control

Mediation will allow you and your spouse to craft the details of your divorce yourselves—including custody and visitation, alimony, child support, and other related matters—instead of having a judge make these determinations for you. In traditional litigation, disputed matters are argued before a judge, evidence is presented, and the judge then issues a decision. There is a risk in going to court, in that no one can say for sure what the result will be of doing so. Judges have great latitude in determining what is "fair and reasonable." Likewise, there are many factors that judges can base their decisions on when deciding what is in the children's "best interests."

Although spouses may make specific requests as to what they would like the judge to order during their hearing, the judge does not necessarily have to grant either party's wishes. It is not unusual for both spouses to be upset with at least some part of the court's ruling. Mediation, on the other hand, avoids the uncertainty and risk associated with going to trial.

Types of Mediators

There are generally two categories of mediators: attorneys and other professionals. Since divorce is a legal process, mediators are most commonly attorneys, but they may also come from different professional backgrounds. Many of these professionals come from the mental health field and include family therapists, social workers, and psychologists, while others may be financial advisors (especially those who have extra training in divorce finances and planning) or clergy members. Regardless of professional background, the person who will mediate your divorce should be a trained mediator. Mediation skills learned in training are required to conduct a successful mediation, and there is a mediation process that needs to be understood and followed by your mediator.

Attorney Mediators

If you choose a mediator who is an attorney, it is important to understand that this attorney is not representing you or your spouse in your divorce. The attorney is acting as a mediator only, and the duties of mediators differ from the duties of personal lawyers in a legal proceeding. Mediators cannot offer legal advice or advocate for either spouse, even if they are attorneys. Attorney mediators can usually prepare all the paperwork that will be required by the court for the dissolution of a marriage once the parties have reached an agreement and mediation has come to a close.

Non-Attorney Mediators

Non-attorney mediators are unable to prepare legal documents. At the conclusion of the mediation process with a non-attorney mediator, the parties are usually referred to an attorney who can prepare the paperwork and finalize the process. Alternatively, the spouses may choose to prepare the paperwork themselves based on the agreements reached during mediation. Regardless, the non-attorney mediator normally provides an outline or summary of the agreed upon terms reached during mediation to assist both parties.

Choosing a Mediator

You will need to discuss the possibility of mediation with your spouse. Your spouse will need to agree to explore mediation as a possibility. If mediation is an option for you and your spouse, you need to find a mediator. You should refer to the tips in Chapter 1 (see page 9) for finding an attorney, as these same tips apply to finding a mediator. To summarize the advice: You may ask other attorneys you have worked with and like, you may ask friends or family members if they might have recommendations, and you may conduct an online search for mediators in your area.

Unlike hiring an attorney to represent you in traditional litigation, you and your spouse will hire your mediator together. This will likely require a joint effort in both the search for and selection of a mediator. It is best that you both meet with a mediator for a consultation to be sure you are both comfortable with this person. You may decide to meet with several mediators before making a final decision. Some questions to ask during the consultation include:

- What is the mediator's process?
- What are the fees involved and will a retainer be required?
- What will be expected of you both during sessions?
- What information may you need to provide?
- How will the mediator handle disagreements?
- How much experience does the mediator have with mediation? What qualifications does the mediator have?
- How much experience does the mediator have with litigation? The answer to this question may be useful, as someone familiar with litigation may know how local courts typically rule on certain issues, and what kind of information a judge will consider relevant. A mediator without any experience in litigation, however, may find it easier to explore nontraditional options to issues that arise in mediation.

- How will sessions be scheduled? How long will a typical session be? How frequently will sessions be held?

- How will communications with the mediator outside of sessions be handled?

- Does the mediator work with or refer clients to any other professionals who may be needed? For example, a mediator may need to bring in a therapist or family counselor to address child custody or childcare concerns properly.

- Can the mediator prepare all the paperwork required in connection with a divorce?

- Can the mediator calculate child support pursuant to child support guidelines?

- If the mediator cannot prepare certain items, will you be referred to a professional who can?

- If the mediator refers you to other professionals, how will the associated fees be handled?

- Based on the issues discussed during your initial consultation, how many sessions does the mediator expect your matter to take? What steps will have to be taken after your final session to complete the process? How long will it take after your final session to complete the process?

- Should you file for divorce before mediation, while going through mediation, or after mediation has ended? Your non-attorney mediator should refer you to an attorney to explain your options and the pros and cons of each.

Mediation Considerations

While there are many benefits to mediation, it is also important to consider its possible pitfalls. Mediation can be a worthwhile process, but it is not for everyone. Before choosing to enter into mediation, keep the following considerations in mind:

- Mediation is best suited to couples who are both motivated to reach a successful outcome and willing to act in good faith. In mediation, each party trusts that the other is fully disclosing all assets and income. If you do not have a strong handle on your marital finances or trust that your spouse will be forthcoming, then mediation may not be the right path for you.

- Mediation requires both parties to participate fully and be confident enough to state their wishes and concerns. Unlike traditional litigation, mediation does not involve personal attorneys to speak for their clients. If you think you will be unable to advocate for yourself, then mediation may not be the right path for you.

- As previously stated, mediation demands a lot of work from both spouses. It requires concentration, the capacity to think clearly and logically, good communication skills, and the ability to recall the details of prior discussions. Any substance abuse condition or mental illness that might impair either party from fully participating or following through with the requirements of mediation may indicate that mediation would not be the right choice in your case.

- While mediation is less expensive than traditional litigation, if it is unsuccessful for any reason and you then have to go through traditional litigation to resolve your matter, the overall cost of getting divorced will end up being higher than pursuing litigation alone would have been. Furthermore, due to the confidentiality of mediation, the mediator will not be able to pass on any information that was discussed during mediation. As such, if the mediator is an attorney, this individual will be disqualified from representing either spouse going forward.

Not all mediations are successful. Mediations that do not result in a full divorce agreement are usually considered unsuccessful. This can happen due to a simple inability to agree on one or more terms of the divorce. Agreements require compromise and creativity in order to satisfy the needs of both parties. Even with a skilled mediator's assistance, sometimes spouses just can't find a solution that would be acceptable to both of them.

During mediation, one spouse may decide to discontinue the process. Mediation may be terminated by either spouse or the mediator for any reason. For example, a mediator may terminate the process if one or both spouses are not complying with the rules of mediation. Regardless of the reason, it is important to understand that mediation can be unsuccessful.

COLLABORATIVE DIVORCE

The other non-adversarial divorce option is called *collaborative divorce*. Think of it as a hybrid between traditional mediation and traditional litigation but with much more weight placed on the mediation process. You would still have your divorce mediated, but you and your spouse would also be represented by separate attorneys who would participate in mediation sessions. In addition, a joint financial professional (sometimes called a "financial specialist") and a joint family therapist (sometimes called a "mental health professional" or "coach") will also participate in the process.

Joint Family Therapist

A *joint family therapist* coordinates the collaborative process. It is important to note that this professional will not provide either spouse with individualized therapy. This professional simply assists spouses with the emotional aspects of the dissolution of their marriage, offers tools to help them communicate effectively, and facilitates a parenting plan if necessary. A joint family therapist may also address the reasons for the breakdown of a marriage and the impacts of this breakdown. A joint family therapist's primary focus, however, is how best to keep a couple on track during this difficult time and move forward.

Joint Financial Professional

A *joint financial professional* (often a financial planner or accountant) helps to gather financial information, assists in completing the financial affidavit (a required document to be filed with the court), identifies the couple's current financial position, and helps the couple plan for their future financial needs. A joint financial professional will normally begin by assessing how much the spouses know in regard to their household finances. If one spouse is the primary handler of financial matters and the other is not familiar with the household finances, then the first order of business will be to gather whatever documentation may be necessary to bring the uninformed spouse up to speed.

A joint financial professional will address any questions either spouse may have about financial disclosures. It may be that one party is concerned that money has been spent or debt has been incurred by the other party. It is the financial professional who will review such concerns with both spouses and obtain further documentation and explanations, if necessary, from each spouse. The end goal at this stage is that each party is made fully aware of the financial history of the marriage.

A joint financial professional will help spouses to identify what their current financial position is and whether any changes should be made at the present time. Are all their bills being paid? Does one of them need access to funds? Is there some "financial bleeding" that can be managed? Once the current finances are dealt with, the financial professional will assist the spouses in determining what post-divorce life will look like financially. Many expenses increase following divorce due to the need to maintain two separate households. Having a good sense of what your post-divorce financial responsibilities will be can help you and your spouse to negotiate your divorce agreement.

Attorneys

Personal attorneys will provide spouses with legal advice to help them negotiate an agreement. They will also rely on the information and assistance provided by the family therapist and the financial professional. These attorneys are also there to calculate child support and draft and review documents. They will explain all the rights and obligations outlined in the written divorce agreement and file all the required paperwork with the court to finalize the divorce.

The Collaborative Divorce Process

In a collaborative divorce, the spouses meet with each professional, usually beginning with the family therapist. These professionals will communicate with each other when necessary to coordinate their services. At regular intervals, and additionally when necessary, these professionals will come together to collaborate with the couple in group meetings.

Collaboration may focus on certain terms of the divorce that need to be negotiated, or perhaps an immediate situation that needs to be addressed (e.g., a new expense, a parenting issue, etc.). All participants in group meetings are normally notified of meetings and the topics to be covered during these meetings in advance, and participants typically agree not to introduce topics at meetings that were not mentioned beforehand, thus avoiding any surprises. Spouses and professionals may be asked to bring certain documents to a meeting, and each spouse's attorney may be there to provide assistance. Prior to a meeting, one of the professionals will be designated as the note-taker, and a summary of the meeting will be provided to all participants shortly after its conclusion.

Once a full agreement is reached on all issues and communicated between all parties, one of the attorneys will prepare a draft agreement for the other attorney to review and modify if necessary. Once the agreement has been written to both attorneys' satisfaction, it is presented to both parties and reviewed again in full before being signed and filed.

If an agreement has been reached, the parties may have the option of waiving a court appearance and requesting that the court accept the paperwork "on the papers." Your attorney will let you know if this option is available in your state and in your case. Assuming all is in order and the court has no questions, a judge will usually review the paperwork and grant the divorce according to the agreement provided within a short time. Your attorney will receive notice and inform you that your divorce has been finalized. If you have to appear in person for your divorce, the review will take place in court before a judge, and your divorce will likely be granted at that time.

The purpose of using shared professionals (family therapist and financial professional) is that it allows the parties to get mutual assistance from a mutual provider by agreement. In litigation, trust is usually at a minimum and each party has their own expert for all issues, sometimes with very different opinions, resulting in increased costs, court involvement, a good deal of uncertainty, and often less optimal outcomes. Conversely, these joint professionals are working for both of you in an open forum. The idea is that you will obtain information together and work together to reach the best agreement possible for you and your children. The use of these joint professionals to do some of the work usually done by an attorney in traditional litigation can also save on costs.

To my knowledge, it is often the case that family therapists and financial professionals have lower hourly rates than attorneys. The more work they can do in their respective fields instead of your attorney doing the work, the lower the cost to you. An attorney in traditional litigation can spend a lot of time on financial discovery and analysis.

Attorneys must frequently try to manage the emotional upheaval their clients are going through. A family therapist can better assist the parties with their feelings and in their communication, allowing the attorneys to focus their time on legal matters while also helping the clients to assist the attorney.

Choosing a Collaborative Divorce Team

Any professional in the collaborative process can assist in forming the rest of the team. Some professionals are members of pre-established groups that have made a commitment to work together. Some professionals build teams as needed. Quite often, one spouse learns of this process and reaches out to a potential member of the team—usually an individual attorney who will represent this spouse, or a mental health professional to which this spouse has been referred. After obtaining more information about the process and deciding to explore it, they may discuss it with their spouse. In the alternative, the team member they spoke with may write a letter to the spouse. Assuming the other spouse is agreeable to trying the collaborative divorce process, the professional originally contacted will assist the spouses in obtaining the rest of the team members. Spouses will be informed of the professionals on the team and have an opportunity to meet everyone at the initial group meeting prior to moving forward officially.

Collaborative Divorce Considerations

Collaborative divorce, like traditional mediation, is a voluntary process. Unlike traditional mediation, however, all participants in a collaborative divorce must sign a contract committing to the process and its rules. The main rules, in general, are as follows:

- Commit to full disclosure of all relevant financial and custodial information as requested or needed.

- Commit to doing everything reasonably possible in the collaborative process to reach a successful outcome, which may be seen as having reached solutions that are acceptable to both participants without court intervention, adversarial techniques, or litigation.

- Commit to retaining all outside professionals jointly and requiring all such professionals to work in a collaborative effort.

- Commit to prioritizing and promoting the children's best interests and not involving them in any negotiations.

- Acknowledge that while the respective attorneys are committing to the process of collaborative divorce, they have a professional duty to diligently represent their individual client and not the other.

- Acknowledge that both a family therapist and financial professional will be jointly hired and paid for by the parties as part of this process, and that neither has provided or will provide individual or joint services for the parties prior to or after this collaborative process.

- Commit to protecting the privacy, respect, and dignity of all involved; conduct yourself with integrity (including correcting any known mistakes or omissions by others); and participate in good faith.

- Acknowledge that the attorneys will immediately withdraw from the process upon knowledge of any knowing lack of disclosure or misrepresentation by their client or knowledge that their client is not participating in the process in good faith.

If it is discovered that someone has violated the rules of collaborative divorce, then the process will likely be stopped. If the process ends prematurely for any reason, all professional participants, including the attorneys, will be prohibited from becoming involved in any future litigation between the parties in connection with the dissolution of their marriage. These rules are there to ensure that participants try their best and act in good faith to reach an amicable settlement.

CONCLUSION

There is a lot to consider when deciding which type of divorce process might be right for you and your spouse. Each type has its pros and cons. Both mediation and collaborative divorce require much more spousal involvement than traditional litigation, but there are more inherent protections for spouses in traditional litigation than there are in the other processes. Traditional mediation offers spouses the most control over costs, while collaborative divorce offers the parties the most specialized assistance and possibly the most creative solutions. In the end, the goal of both mediation and collaborative divorce is to reach a lasting agreement as efficiently and amicably as possible.

In mediation and collaborative divorce, spouses bear the burden of reaching an agreement. It may not be an easy task to accomplish, but it is a worthwhile one. As one of my clients once noted, "As difficult as it may seem, if you can take away the emotionality of the situation and identify the things that are most important to you, and those things that are most important to your spouse, it's possible to turn an incredibly challenging endeavor into one that can have a decent outcome."

6.

Regarding Children

The process of going through a divorce is not normally easy for either spouse, but it can be even more difficult for the spouses' children. If you are a parent who is getting divorced, it is important to be aware of the emotional rollercoaster your children may experience as a result, and crucial to be prepared to be there for your children. You are primarily responsible for protecting your children in the face of divorce, helping them to cope with the divorce process and the changes to the family unit that come from divorce. Learning how your parental rights can be impacted by divorce and understanding the challenges of children navigating two separate households are good first steps to take in this situation.

In most divorce cases, the court handles these matters by requiring all parents going through divorce to attend a parental education class, no matter the ages of their children. This class does not focus on how to take care of or raise children, but rather on what children commonly go through during the divorce process, what you can do to help them, and what actions you should avoid so as not to harm them. The length of the class and the manner in which you may take it varies from state to state. You and your spouse may be excused from taking the class if you are participating in a collaborative divorce or receiving some other comparable counselling. You can obtain a list of providers from your attorney or online.

If you have children under the age of eighteen, you'll have to plan for your post-divorce future with them mind. This means having discussions and negotiations with your spouse about parenting time, decision making, caretakers, travel, and living arrangements. If you reach an agreement on these issues, the agreed-upon terms will be put in writing, most likely accepted by the judge, and made an order of the court, which will require both parties to follow these terms. Courts prefer that issues regarding children be addressed as soon as possible and will gladly accept agreed-upon terms of parenting even if the financial aspects of a divorce have not yet been settled.

If you and your spouse are unable to reach an agreement in regard to your children, then your case will eventually be reviewed by the court to determine the type of intervention needed to assist you in reaching an agreement. If there is still no agreement after attempts to resolve the issues between you and your spouse, the court will decide upon the matter after a hearing.

This chapter will first address the different types of child custody and then review your parenting plan options. It will then discuss issues to be aware of when making parenting schedules and what to expect in the event of a disagreement that requires court assistance. Keep in mind that the exact terms used to address different custody and parenting plans may vary from state to state. There may also be slight variations in how courts implement these issues.

LEGAL CUSTODY

Legal custody refers to the right to be informed of and participate in any major decision affecting the health, education, or welfare of your child. This right is broad and covers many subjects about which parents routinely make decisions for their children, including the type of medical care a child receives, what school a child attends, which religion a child follows (if any), what disciplinary measures a child might face, when a child might be allowed to obtain a driver's license, etc.

By and large, most parents share *joint legal custody* of their children following a divorce—that is, they both have the legal right to participate in the types of decisions mentioned in the last paragraph. In this case, parents must do their best to make such decisions together. If they cannot do so, or if one parent makes a major decision without consulting the other, than the other parent may file a motion with the court and ask the judge to address the issue.

PHYSICAL CUSTODY

Physical custody is a term that refers to where a child lives. When a child resides primarily with one parent, that parent is said to have *primary physical custody*. In situations in which a child spends equal or near equal amounts of time with each parent, the parents are said to have *shared physical custody*. If a divorced couple has multiple children, in a majority of cases, all of them will be on the same schedule, spending time with each parent together. There are, however, instances in which siblings are not on the same schedule—that is, one (or less than all) is with one parent while the other (or others) is with the other parent. The term for this arrangement is *split physical custody*. The day-to-day and week-to-week schedule of a child with each parent is normally detailed in writing and referred to as a *parenting plan*. The parenting plan determines whether someone has primary physical custody, shared physical custody, or split physical custody.

Many people think that physical custody determines child support. While it is true that the parent who has primary physical custody is usually entitled to receive child support from the other parent, this is not always the case. Shared and split physical custody, despite common assumptions to the contrary, does not mean that no one pays child support. It is often the case that child support is still due one parent. The finances of the parents, in addition to the residency of the child, is considered and factored into the determination of who pays child support and in what amount. (See Chapter 7 on page 87 for more information on child support.)

PARENTING PLANS

One size does not fit all when it comes to parenting plans. Of course, there are some basic similarities when it comes to the options parents and the courts consider. A major determining factor when courts and child advocates consider a post-divorce plan is maintaining consistency for the children. Parents often move towards plans that resemble the type of care they provided for the children during their marriage. This does not mean, however, that parents or the court cannot choose something different than the status quo—especially if the status quo would not be in the best interests of the children.

Primary Physical Custody

Parenting plans still include the "traditional" option of primary physical custody, in which the children live with one parent, who is considered the primary caregiver, most of the time. Parenting time with the other parent usually includes alternate weekends, with one or two weeknight visits, or a weeknight overnight. Weekends may be defined as Saturday and Sunday, or they may start on Friday evening and go through Monday morning. The exact schedule is negotiable and will depend on what is right for your family. These plans are often born out of necessity and continue what was customary during the marriage.

Often the noncustodial parent was not the "primary" parent, due to a work schedule that often included travel or long hours. Sometimes parties choose the traditional plan due to cultural beliefs or personal preference. Other times, this plan is chosen because one of the parents could not or would not take on the responsibilities of primary caregiver. Regardless, if this plan serves the children's best interests, then there is no reason it should not be chosen simply because it is "traditional."

Be sure to make the choices that are best for your family and not be influenced by the opinions of others. Just because one parent is considered the "primary" parent (now more often referred to as the "residential" parent), this does not make the other parent less important. It's the quality of time spent that matters most, not the quantity. Likewise, it is important to note that "parenting time" and "visitation" refer to the same thing. Over the years, there has been a move away from the use of the term "visitation" and towards "parenting time" by attorneys and the courts—even when we are referring to time a nonresidential parent spends with the children. We recognize that parents are not "visiting" their children, they are parenting them.

Divorce sometimes leads the parent who has not traditionally been "primary" to seek "primary" status. Sometimes this decision results from the urging of a third party (often the spouse's new partner or the spouse's parent). The parent may wish to be perceived by the court, extended family members, and others as being more involved with the children than is perhaps the case. The parent may be attempting to avoid paying child support or gain bargaining power over the financial negotiations. Regardless, any attempt to negotiate a parenting plan or custodial arrangement that is not based solely on what is best for the children is misguided.

Shared Physical Custody

Shared physical custody divides the time with the children between the parents more evenly. This arrangement was born out of an increase in the number of families in which both parents are employed and consequently share childcare duties more equally. A shared custody schedule often mimics what was customary during the marriage and provides consistency for the children going forward.

The schedule can take various forms in shared custody. Children may spend one whole week with one parent and then the next week with the other. But most children split the week between parents, spending half the week with one parent and half the week with the other. There are, of course, a number of possible ways to split the week. Some children keep the same days (for instance, Sunday through Wednesday afternoon with one parent, and Wednesday afternoon through Saturday with the other), while others rotate days and alternate whole weekends. Your attorney or mediator can review the various plans with you to help you determine what would work best for your family.

This type of arrangement works best when the parents reside close together, since there is likely to be more regular movement of the children from one home to the other. If the parties expect to live far apart, then the travel the children will have to endure between parents needs to be considered when weighing this option. Moreover, parents must also determine what school the children will attend and consider how shared physical custody will impact travel time to this school.

Split Physical Custody

Although rare, this type of parenting plan does exist. For whatever reason, the parents or the judge may decide it is in the best interests of the children to experience a majority of parenting time separately from their siblings. Perhaps there is a great divide in the ages of the children. Perhaps one child has a medical issue that requires a lot of attention. Maybe there is a serious rift between siblings or another problematic family dynamic that impairs parenting the children together. The manner in which the children are divided and the exact schedules they will have with each parent should be determined on a case-by-case basis. Your attorney or mediator can provide more information and options if needed.

BEYOND THE BASICS

Beyond the week-to-week schedule, parents need to plan for holidays, vacations, and other special events. They need to agree upon transportation of the children from home to home. They may also need to agree upon the type and frequency of communication between themselves and with their children while the children are with the other parent. They may plan for unexpected events such as a change in a child's schedule or not being able to parent according to the schedule for any number of reasons.

Holidays

By and large, most parents choose to alternate major holidays and rotate them from year to year. Some choose to divide and share special days each year. You need to do what makes the most sense for you and your family. Make a list of all the holidays that are important to your family. Think about how you and your children have celebrated these holidays in the past. What is important to you? What is important to your spouse? What traditions would be important to try to retain for your children? Will travel be required to visit extended family? These are the things that should guide you when trying to determine a fair holiday schedule.

Once you've got a list of holidays, determine the days and hours each will include. You don't have limit holidays to their dates on the calendar. For instance, Thanksgiving could include just Thanksgiving Day, or it may begin upon the children's dismissal from school on the Wednesday immediately preceding the holiday and end sometime after the holiday (Friday, Saturday, Sunday, or even Monday morning). Alternatively, the holiday may be divided and shared, with the children being with one parent from Wednesday after school through Thursday, and the other parent from Friday to Saturday or Sunday. When it comes to who gets the kids on the actual Thursday holiday, parents could rotate each year.

Understand that holidays take precedence over the regular parenting plan. That is, the regular schedule will be suspended for holiday time. Once holiday time is over, the regular schedule will resume. Don't try to figure out how to "make up" time lost due to another parent's holiday. Constant changes to the schedule often confuse everyone. Each parent will periodically "lose" time due to holidays, vacations, or special events of the other. It usually all washes out in the end. Please don't let the necessary schedule changes be a source of stress. Make the most of your holiday celebrations with your children and let them enjoy holidays with their other parent as well.

Vacations

Just like with holidays, the number and length of vacations with the children should be discussed and agreed upon with your spouse. Vacations, like holidays, will interrupt the regular parenting schedule. How many weeks will you each be able to take? Can weeks be taken consecutively? Will you and your spouse alter school vacation weeks or divide them? Perhaps you may choose to follow the regular parenting schedule during some or all school breaks. How much advanced notice of vacation should you give the other parent? Vacation plans during summer break may need to be determined early in the year so as to coordinate summer camps or other childcare options in a timely manner.

Registration and deposits for summer activities often need to be settled in advance. What if you and your spouse want the same summer weeks? Should you identify who has first choice in odd years and in even years in the event of a conflict? Should the parent who has first choice be required to specify desired weeks by a certain date? Itineraries of travel with children are normally expected to be shared between parents, but what information specifically should be included? Will there be any limitations on types of travel or travel destinations? Do your children have passports? If not, will you and your spouse agree to cooperate in obtaining them if needed?

Significant Others

For some, discussions may also involve current or future significant others. This may be especially difficult if the current significant other is in some way associated with the breakdown of the marriage. A parent's new romantic partner can be a struggle for children to accept. Children often resist a new person as a way of protecting their other parent. They may be jealous of the new partner and wonder if they will be replaced by this person's kids, or by kids that may come as a result of this new romantic pairing. It's natural for young children to ask questions about the new person in mommy or daddy's life. Children not only have to

Avoiding Conflicts in Scheduling

It can be a bit daunting to have to think about holidays and school vacations in this way. Rarely does anyone want to do it, especially if things are cordial with the other parent, but it is better to have a detailed schedule that you can rely on in the event of a disagreement, or if things between you and your spouse become contentious in the future. It will reduce the likelihood of arguments around the holidays and provide some certainty for your children. Working hard on deliberations, negotiations, and decision making to arrive at a schedule in advance is better than going back to court at a later date to settle these issues after a dispute has arisen. Few people, if any, enjoy going back to litigation or even mediation. You may also wish to also include the following considerations in your parenting plan:

- Advance notice for foreseeable changes to the parenting plan, which can refer to small matters, such as changes in pick-up or drop-off times, to big issues, such as changes in days or weekends.

- Right of first refusal. In other words, if the parent who is supposed to be with the children is unable to take them, that parent must give the other parent the first opportunity to care for the children before obtaining other childcare.

- Relocation of residence. How much written notice must one parent give the other in the event of an anticipated change in residence location? How far can a parent go in terms of miles, driving time, or counties without needing to change the parenting plan? Will the children be restricted to residing in a certain state?

deal with their own feelings, but they also have to navigate the other parent's reaction to this new relationship.

Also keep in mind that your children's timeframe regarding acceptance of the divorce may be different from yours. It is likely that you or your spouse acknowledged and came to terms with the dissolution of your marriage (or will do so) much sooner than your children. Some children will hold on to the hope that their parents will eventually reconcile

REGARDING CHILDREN 75

- Identifying schools or religious programs, or any medical treatment or medical providers for the children.
- For children who are not yet in school, identifying which parent's residence will determine the children's school district.
- Acknowledgment of agreed-upon activities for the children.
- Acknowledgement that changes in the parenting plan may be necessary for special events, and that good faith efforts to accommodate such changes should be made when they are warranted.
- Agreement on pick-up and drop-off locations and associated transportation.
- Acknowledgment that "parent" tickets for certain school or extracurricular events will be distributed equally or according to mutual agreement.
- How communication with the other parent will be handled when children are staying with one of their parents.
- Acknowledgment that the parent who has custody of the children on school days is also responsible for the children completing their assigned schoolwork.
- Identifying the preferred method of communication between parents for non-emergency child-related issues.

Ideally, you will put together a detailed parenting plan with your spouse and then put it in a drawer and never have to look at it again. As long as you both agree, you can follow any schedule you would like that works for your children.

even after the divorce has been finalized. While you may be anxious to "get on" with your life, your children may still be mourning the loss of the family unit as it once was. In such a situation, it is important to explore ways to manage this process. Perhaps you and your spouse could agree to notify each other before introducing your children to a new romantic partner. This way you can be prepared to answer any questions your children may have on the subject. Some parents agree to allow the other to meet the new individual. This is done as a courtesy, not for the purpose of vetting or accepting the person. Some parents also agree in writing not to refer to anyone else—or encourage the children to refer to anyone else—as "Mom" or "Dad." Depending on the ages of your children, it may be helpful to discuss how you will each refer to a new partner. Will you simply use the person's name, or will you use a term such as "friend," "best friend," "girlfriend," "boyfriend," or "significant other"?

You and your spouse may find it helpful to consult a family therapist to assist in identifying and managing other concerns surrounding this topic. If your spouse will not go, then you may still go by yourself. A good parenting professional will provide you with coping strategies and advice to help your child manage the changing family dynamic. Your attorney or mediator should be able to guide you in finding such a professional. It is important to understand that any common ground you can establish on this front will help to defuse potential arguments and eliminate unwanted surprises—all for the benefit of your children.

CHILD-CENTRIC PLANNING

Many people forget the obvious when they're embroiled in their divorce: It is the children, for the most part, who are going to be traveling back and forth in accordance with the parenting plan. In general, you want to try to minimize this travel. You also need to be considerate of the children's schedules and needs during their non-school time, especially as they get older. They may have jobs, extracurricular activities such as sports or music lessons, or social activities they want to attend. Build flexibility into your plan and be prepared to follow through without too much fuss. Children don't count the hours with a parent, but they do note the disruption in their lives that transitions cause, and they remember the quality of the time they have spent with each parent.

It is important to look at any proposed parenting plan from your child's perspective. Often parents are consumed with how the divorce is affecting them. As such, they sometimes negotiate a plan that may seem fair to them or a plan that works with their schedule, not realizing that what they've come up with may be very difficult or unfair to their children. Take a moment now and think about your child's daily routine.

- How do they handle transitions? While it is usually best to minimize their exchanges between parents, children who do not transition well may need even more consideration in regard to this matter. Perhaps fewer transitions and longer periods of parenting time with one parent would be beneficial. Perhaps more visits by the noncustodial parent to the custodial parent's house, allowing the child to avoid having to switch households would be helpful. Similar consideration should be given to children who have a hard time dealing with long separations from a parent. Each child is different and sometimes the best option is to take a slightly varied schedule for each child, depending on each child's needs or age. Failing to do so may result in an impasse and thus a need to rework the parenting plan, hindering the ability of everyone to move forward.

- What activities are they already committed to? While time with parents is certainly important, it is equally important not only to recognize but also, to some extent, respect what children choose to do in their free time. Many children participate in sports or other structured extracurricular activities, which can be very time consuming and involve travel. Creating a schedule that ignores these commitments can result in over-scheduled children or prevent children from attending these activities, both of which are undesirable outcomes.

- How can traveling be minimized? Most people find traveling on a regular basis difficult. And usually, the longer the commute, the more there is to complain about. Keep this idea in mind for yourself and your children.

- Will the parenting plan have a negative effect on the children's sleep or homework? Avoid transition times that will interfere with bedtime routines for younger children. Give older children enough time to settle in and get homework done before they need to wind down for the night. Choose an alternative to any arrangement that forces a child to wake unreasonably early in the morning, especially on school days.

- Does the schedule include any downtime? A letter I read many years ago, written by a young teen, spoke of the resentment he felt at having to get on an airplane the day after the last day of school to transition to the other parent. While he gave no indication that he did not want to see the other parent, he regretted not having the opportunity to celebrate the end of the school year with his friends. I have since heard similar stories, even from children whose travel involved only a car ride. The familiar thread is the feeling that there is "Mom's time" and "Dad's time" but no "me time."

- Should kids of different ages be on the same schedule? The ages, activities, and temperaments of the children should be taken into consideration.
- Does the schedule focus on quality time with each parent or just on quantity? Don't argue over hours or even days. Create a schedule in which you can each offer the most of yourselves and have the best chance of getting the best out of your kids.
- Does the schedule allow for deviations in connection with a child's reasonable wants or needs?

GETTING INPUT FROM THE CHILDREN

Depending on your children's ages and maturity levels, their input regarding parenting plans may be warranted. How this is done—and if it is done at all—will depend upon the circumstances of your case. This decision should be mutual and any such discussion with the children should be held by both parents together. One parent should not discuss the divorce, including any proposed parenting plans, with the children without the consent of the other parent. If children have any serious concerns about a proposed schedule in terms of how it might affect such important matters as their relationships with their parents, their schooling, their activities, or their sleep patterns, then these issues should be discussed between the parents. Perhaps the schedule can be reworked with these concerns in mind.

It is important to distinguish between obtaining feedback from a mature child and allowing the child to become involved in negotiating a parenting plan. The child should not be allowed or encouraged to lobby for certain parenting terms on behalf of one parent. Likewise, it would not be appropriate simply to ask children what they would like in regard to a parenting plan arrangement or where they would like to live. Doing so would give the children too much control, put the children in the middle of their parents' dispute, and possibly lead to the children harboring feelings of guilt over the parenting plan that has been made. It may also tempt a parent to try to bribe the children. Hard feelings between child and parent can sometimes develop if the child seemed to side with one parent's parenting plan preferences. A rift between siblings can occur if they share different opinions on custody and parenting. Children may use their perceived sense of control to manipulate situations involving their parents in the future. None of these scenarios are in the best interests of the children.

CUSTODY DISPUTES

It may be that you and your spouse cannot agree on custody or a parenting plan. Your disagreements may be significant in nature. Perhaps one parent does not want the other to have joint legal custody, or one parent wants to be the primary parent and the other wants to follow a shared parenting plan. Of course, your disagreement may be less significant in nature. Perhaps the specific days, hours, or holiday time of a parenting plan are in dispute. If negotiations between you and your spouse (or between your respective attorneys) do not result in a resolution of these differences, other parties may be called in to assist in the matter.

You and your spouse may be referred to a family therapist, who can attempt to address parental concerns and help you to reach an agreement. The therapist may come at a cost to you or free of charge through the family services provider of the court. If you are still unable to reach an agreement, then the court will assign your case for a hearing and may take additional measures in order to come to a decision. Depending on the nature of the dispute, sometimes it is necessary for the court to gather outside information about the children or hear from them. The judge will not receive information from your children directly. Your child will not be made to testify in court. Instead, a skilled mental health professional or experienced child advocate will obtain this information.

The judge will likely want to know about your children's health, maturity, general well-being, schedules, interests, and relationships with you and your spouse, as well as their general awareness of your divorce and the associated custodial or parenting plan dispute.

Information pertaining to your children may also be gathered from people who are closely connected to them, such as teachers or other school personnel, medical providers, therapists, family members, neighbors or daycare providers. The judge may appoint a person to acquire this information if requested to do so by either parent, or simply if the judge thinks it would be helpful, and there are a few ways in which this information may be acquired.

Guardian Ad Litem (GAL) and Attorney for Minor Children (AMC)

The judge may appoint a *guardian ad litem*, or *GAL*, which refers to a person who obtains information pertaining to the children and then reports it to the court (through testimony at a hearing), while also offering an opinion on what parenting choices would be in the best interests of the children in light of this information. This individual is often an attorney but does not have to be an attorney. A GAL is typically appointed when there are younger children involved in a divorce.

The judge may appoint an *attorney for minor children*, or *AMC*, which refers to an attorney who obtains information pertaining to the children and then reports it to the court (through testimony at a hearing), while also advising the court on what the children would like in regard to the parenting plan. An AMC is usually appointed when there are older children involved in a divorce.

GALs and AMCs usually share their findings and recommendations with the spouses and the spouses' attorneys prior to the final hearing of a parenting plan or custody matter. It represents the last opportunity for spouses to craft an agreement before allowing the judge to do so. Both GALs and AMCs are private third parties that usually require fees for their services. It is customary for them to bill by the hour and request a retainer, the amount of which is based on the workload expected. If spouses cannot agree on how the costs of this professional should be managed, the judge will determine the issue after reviewing the financial status of each spouse.

Family Services Evaluation

Alternatively, the judge may instead order that an evaluation be performed by the family services division of the court. This is a free service from the court. In this case, your file will be referred to a family therapist, who will obtain information from you, your spouse, your children, and any other relevant sources. Your children will not have to come to court. If information is needed from them, the family relations therapist will normally schedule two home visits—one with you and your children, and one with your spouse and your children.

Once the evaluation is done, the family therapist will schedule a meeting with you, your spouse, and your attorneys to review the evaluation and make recommendations in connection with the custody or parenting issues in dispute. You and your spouse will likely have some time to consider the recommendations, resume negotiations if necessary, and reach an agreement if possible. If no agreement can be reached, then the judge will be notified of the recommendation as part of your custody hearing.

It is ultimately the judge's decision to appoint a GAL or AMC, or to refer your case to family relations or some other court process that may be applicable in your state. The judge also determines the scope of this professional's duties, which may vary from case to case. Your attorney should be able to advise you in regard to whether you should request this type of professional, the circumstances under which this individual may be appointed by the judge, and the process and costs involved with this service.

It is important to note that, although this professional is appointed by the judge, the judge is not obligated to rule in accordance with this person's recommendations. The judge will consider all the evidence when making these important decisions.

SOLE LEGAL CUSTODY

Occasionally, one parent is given *sole legal custody* of the children. In other words, only this parent is allowed to make major decisions in regard to the children. Sole legal custody can happen for a number of reasons. A parent can lose the right to have input in their children's lives if they have previously refused to take part in making common parenting decisions, which include decisions on regular care providers, medical providers (as well as the type of medical care children receive), the children's schooling, the children's religious practices, disciplinary measures, internet usage, and employment as teens.

Perhaps one parent does not care to have custody and trusts the other parent to make the right choices. Perhaps this parent does not respond to inquiries from the other parent in a timely manner or has failed to act in the best interests of the children. It may be that there is a medical condition or substance abuse issue that impairs a parent's ability to make appropriate decisions. Another reason a judge may order sole legal custody to one parent is that co-parenting has been found not to be in the best interest of the children. Sometimes fighting between parents over parenting decisions causes such disruption in their children's lives that taking away one parent's rights to legal custody is deemed more desirable than allowing both parents to continue parenting jointly.

If sole legal custody is ordered, it is often the case that the parent allowed to make parenting decisions still has the obligation to inform the other parent of the decisions being made. Not having legal custody is not the same as termination of parental rights. A parent who does not have legal custody still may have the right to parenting time with his or her children. Likewise, child support, if required, will still be due from a parent who does not have legal custody.

HYBRID OPTION

There is a hybrid option for legal custody that is sometimes agreed upon by parents and sometimes, although less often, ordered by a judge. It is characterized by parents sharing joint legal custody but, in the event that they are unable to agree on a decision despite good faith efforts, one parent having final decision-making authority. Usually this "tie-breaking" ability or "trump card" is given to one parent in all decisions, sometimes it is divided according to specific parenting issues. For example, one parent would have the final decision-making authority in connection with school situations, while the other would have the final decision-making authority in connection with medical situations. Specific designations would need to be discussed between the parties and would depend on the family's circumstances.

SUPERVISED OR SUSPENDED VISITATION

There are instances when the court may require that parenting time be supervised or even suspended. Such decisions are made for the safety of the children. They are meant to shield them from physical, psychological, and emotional harm. Supervised or suspended parenting time is often associated with a parent who has substance abuse issues or mental health issues, which can negatively impact that person's ability to parent

REGARDING CHILDREN

appropriately. It may also result from repeated failure to supervise the children properly, close association by the parent with other people who are deemed a safety concern while with the children (drug users, gang members, convicted child molesters, sex offenders, etc.), or the children's repeated exposure to behavior that is grossly inappropriate. When one parent makes a claim of unfit parenting against the other parent, this claim has to be proved in court. If the court deems the concern valid, then it will likely order parenting time to be supervised or suspended.

Supervised parenting time may take place at a facility that charges for such service, or it may be allowed to take place with a family member or friend of the parent who is under the order of supervised parenting time. Who will be allowed to supervise and under what conditions and for how long such supervised parenting time will last are decisions of the court, and these decisions may be reviewed on a periodic basis or upon a substantial change in circumstances. In some cases, the court may suspend parenting time entirely if the suspension is deemed to be in the best interests of the children. In these cases, there is usually some requirement that needs to be satisfied for parenting time—whether regular or supervised—to resume. It may be that a parent or child has to undergo some sort of therapy or treatment, or perhaps they both must attend reunification therapy if they have been separated for some time. Whatever the circumstances, proof of compliance with the court-ordered requirements and perhaps a recommendation from a mental health provider or child advocate will usually be required for parenting time rights to be reinstated by the court.

FIVE WAYS TO PROTECT YOUR CHILDREN

Please note that the following suggestions are based on my years of firsthand experience in working with clients going through divorce, and from information garnered from countless discussions, articles, and presentations by family therapists and other mental health professionals, pediatricians, attorneys, and other individuals who represent children by appointment of the court.

1. **Never put your children in the middle of your issues.** This is easier said than done, of course, and many otherwise wonderful parents make this mistake. Avoid sharing information about your court case with your children. Do not lead your children into picking sides or

ask them to hide information from their other parent. It's important to control your emotions, take the high road, maintain consistency, and do your very best to co-parent during this very difficult time. Remember that the feelings of hurt, guilt, and anger caused by the breakdown of your marriage can easily blind you to your actions.

2. **Assure, reassure, and re-reassure your children that the break-up is not their fault.** No matter how unreasonable or illogical their conclusions may seem, kids often blame themselves in some way for their parents' divorce. They often think that if they had only acted better, listened more, gotten better grades, or not fought so much with their siblings, then their parents would not be getting divorced. Here's what I've been told helps tremendously: Let them know, together and often, that your decision to end your marriage was not something they caused.

3. **If possible, and if no danger to either spouse's safety exists in doing so, the first discussion of divorce with the children should be held by both parents together.** Since the discussion should be age appropriate, consider having separate talks with your children according to their ages. In other words, both parents can have one conversation with their older children, and then another conversation with their younger children. Presenting a unified front *without blame* is one of the greatest gifts you could give your children in this situation. You may then assure them right from the beginning that the divorce and family restructuring has nothing to do with them, that you will both still be there for them, that you will both do everything possible to protect them from the negative repercussions of divorce, and that they will be okay.

4. **Promptly notify school counselors and other important caregivers of your pending divorce.** These individuals do not need to know any details. The purpose of notification is to have them keep an eye open for any changes in the behavior or development of your children so that these issues may be properly addressed. The more support your children receive during this time, the better. If a child's behavior changes radically, ask to speak to the child's school therapist about it. This person may recommend that your child receive in-school support or outside therapy.

REGARDING CHILDREN

5. **Keep your divorce in perspective.** Leading up to and during your divorce, it is common to feel overwhelmed, as though your life is out of control and your future is frighteningly uncertain. Although the break-up of your marriage will bring about many changes in your life and the effects of divorce will be something you will need to manage going forward, your life will go on. Most people are able to find peace and happiness after divorce. Making a conscious effort to focus on the positive and not dwell on the negative will help you, your spouse, and your children. Children always seem to know more about what their parents are going through than parents think they do. And they often follow their parents' lead in regard to their emotions and how they handle tough situations. Show them that divorce is a problem to be solved, not a battle to be won or lost. Divorce does not have to ruin anyone's life.

ADULT CHILDREN OF DIVORCE

Although there is a wealth of concern and support for minor children of divorce, there is often not much thought given to adult children of divorce. People over the age of eighteen, and even those in their late twenties and thirties, are often negatively affected by their parents' divorce. Their concerns need to be acknowledged and addressed, too. They often worry about younger siblings and spend much of their time providing them with emotional support. It is also not uncommon for adult children to expend a significant amount of energy trying to protect the parent they think is most vulnerable from harm.

In addition, parents, often absorbed in their own grief or new life, not only fail to recognize the effects the divorce is having on their adult children, but also don't think it inappropriate to share details of their divorce with them. Some treat their adult children as friends to confide in, asking them to keep secrets. This is a tremendous burden to put on an adult child. No matter their ages, your children are still your children. Most don't want to take sides or hear bad things about their other parent.

There are, however, some adult children who may want to be involved in the divorce process, or who may wish to help a parent to get through a difficult divorce. In these cases, therapists say it is still important for parents to maintain a parental role. You may accept the support of your adult children while also keeping their needs and feelings—as well as the fact that they are also the children of their other parent—in mind.

CONCLUSION

It is always best for you and your spouse to try to resolve issues regarding your children yourselves. Unresolved issues will be decided by a judge who does not know and will likely never see your children. Unresolved issues may lead to your children becoming involved in the court process and open the door to parenting input from third parties. You and your spouse know your children better than any judge or other third party and are, in all probability, in a better position to craft a parenting plan that is in their best interests. If needed, there will be people who can assist you and your spouse in this process, both in court and out of court. Take advantage of any help you can obtain. Being able to work together and reach an agreement regarding custody and parenting time will be a great gift for your children now and will help form a solid foundation for future co-parenting.

In the end, it is best to ignore the labels various parenting plans are given as well as any negative opinions anyone you know may have of them. Focus instead on how best to take advantage of the strengths and availability of each parent while keeping things as consistent as possible for the children. And if things aren't working out or changes become necessary as your children grow older and schedules change, be open to making these changes. Parenting plans are not meant to be set in stone. They, like your parenting, will need to evolve with your children and life circumstances.

7.

Money Matters

As this book's previous chapters have described, there are several major concerns when it comes to divorce. While children are a chief concern in divorce, another is almost always money. Whether or not you have an income, divorce can impact your financial life. It is understandable that you would be concerned about what your finances might look like during and after the divorce process, and it is natural to turn to the person representing you, your lawyer, for answers. You will likely want your attorney to predict how property will be divided, how income may have to be shared, and how expenses will be paid during the divorce process. While your attorney can give you some general information on how these matters are decided, there will probably not be enough information available at the beginning of your divorce for any accurate predictions to be made. It will not be until much later in the proceedings, when your lawyer has had the benefit of discovery and been given much more information from you regarding your marital finances, that any predictions can be made with any confidence.

The first order of business will be for you and your spouse to prepare and exchange a financial disclosure statement, which I'll refer to as a financial affidavit. It may be referred to by a different name in your state. It is required to be completed and filed with the court in most divorces. As this chapter will explain, this affidavit will play an important role in determining the final financial orders of your divorce, including orders regarding child support, alimony, property, and debt allocation.

FINANCIAL AFFIDAVIT

A *financial affidavit* is a complete list of your income, expenses, assets, and debts. You must sign and date it, swear to its accuracy, and have it notarized. The financial affidavit is a basic snapshot of your financial situation and is often periodically updated as a divorce progresses. It is extremely important to be as accurate as possible when completing this document. Many attorneys utilize a form created by the court for this purpose, but some use other versions. Regardless of the form used, it will contain an extensive list of all types of income, assets, expenses, and debts, which will make it a helpful reference for you to have.

The information contained in this form will be relied upon heavily by both the court and the attorneys when analyzing and making financial recommendations or decisions. Other information provided as part of the discovery process may confirm or supplement the information provided in financial affidavits. Most attorneys conduct basic audits—that is, examinations—of the financial information they receive. Ideally, the supplemental information from you and your spouse will match the information contained in both your financial affidavits. Inconsistencies may warrant further inspection or additional disclosure, or they may lead to a more thorough audit conducted by an outside professional hired by your or your spouse's attorney.

Breaking Down Your Financials

Completing a financial affidavit can be a bit tricky, and most people require assistance in doing so. Although the court form will likely include lengthy written instructions on how to fill it out, you may still have questions. Your attorney can help you, and you should follow your attorney's advice. Nevertheless, there are a few general tips that may prove useful in connection with common aspects of a financial affidavit.

Income

You are required to list your income from all sources. Self-employed individuals usually have the hardest time with this part. Their income is often inconsistent, and they may not even know how to calculate it accurately, often relying on an accountant to do so at the end of each year. It is usually appropriate for self-employed people to use an average of their income, after tax deductible business expenses, over the past fifty-two weeks. Rental income should also be listed after allowable tax deductions. Your bookkeeper or accountant should be able to assist you with these numbers. For retirees, there are line items for social security and other types of income that may be applicable.

Expenses

You are required to list all your expenses. Difficulty often arises in regard to the form of this required information. Some states require you to list monthly expenses, some require you to list weekly expenses, and some let you decide how to list them. Be sure to provide the correct information and be consistent if given the option. Those who are familiar with their household expenses usually know their monthly expenses and often list this amount instead of their weekly amount, which may be in error. Don't forget to include costs that you may not pay monthly, such as car or life insurance. Some pay these and other expenses on a quarterly or yearly basis, and will not only need to include them on the financial disclosure but also have to convert the payment to the monthly or weekly amount, as required. Discretionary expenses as well as many personal expenses and children's expenses are often incurred sporadically and may not be items that are accounted for in the budget and, consequently, not well known. Go through your financial records (and memory) so that you may provide accurate estimates for these types of expenses. It is important to provide a good accounting of your actual expenditures so that they can be taken into consideration when determining future finances.

The next issue commonly encountered in the process of filling out a financial affidavit is how to list expenses that are paid jointly. If you divide certain expenses (for example, you pay the cell phone bill and your spouse pays the electric bill), then list the bills you pay at 100 percent and note the bills your spouse pays. If you both contribute funds to a bank account from which the bills are paid, then you can either list all such bills at 50 percent (or whatever percentage you contribute if different than 50 percent) and then note that your spouse pays the other percentage, or you can list all bills at 100 percent with a note that your spouse contributes 50 percent (or whatever percentage your spouse contributes if different than 50 percent) to the household bills.

Notes clarifying the numbers and information you provide will be very helpful, not just in the expense section but throughout the financial affidavit.

Debts

These items usually need to be listed according to title—i.e., whose name is on the debt. (It is important to note, however, that this fact may not determine who will be responsible for the debt in the divorce.) Unless otherwise instructed, a credit card bill that is in your name alone—even if your spouse is an authorized user—should go only on your financial affidavit. Debts in one person's name should usually be listed at 100 percent of the value of these debts. Debts held jointly with your spouse should usually be listed at 50 percent of the value of these debts.

Assets

These items usually need to be listed according to title—i.e., whose name is on the asset. (It is important to note, however, that this fact may not determine who will be entitled to the asset in the divorce.) Unless instructed otherwise, a vehicle that you drive and intend to keep after the divorce but is in your spouse's name alone should go solely on your spouse's financial affidavit. Assets in one person's name should likely be listed at 100 percent of the value of these assets. Assets held jointly with your spouse should likely be listed at 50 percent of the value of these assets (unless the title specifically states otherwise).

There may be a section on a financial affidavit dedicated to household furnishings or "other property," which is almost always a cause for pause. Some people choose to leave this section blank because they, understandably, don't know how to calculate the value of the contents of an entire house or even just a set of tools, for example. Other people list a very high number based on what they remember spending for the contents when new or their figuring out what it would cost to replace the contents. Neither approach is ideal. Instead, you will need to calculate the resale value, or "estate sale" value, of the contents of your household. Have you ever been to an estate sale? Unless it contains highly collectible art or antiques, everything sells for pennies on the dollar. Nevertheless, your household contents have some value. Simply write down a reasonable number. Listing your assets at too high or too low a value would not be in your best interest.

Life Insurance

Life insurance is another area where mistakes are commonly made when it comes to financial affidavits. Unfortunately, the court form may not have a line that distinguishes between a whole life and a term life insurance policy. It may not have a space to note the amount of the death benefit of a policy. As a result, most people list the death benefit as the value of their life insurance policies, which is incorrect. The value is normally zero for term policies. Whole life policies normally have a cash value. The cash value is what should be listed as the value for these policies. Even if it is not required, it is a good idea to add a note listing the amount of the death benefit of each of your life insurance policies. This information is likely to be helpful to your attorney or the judge in the future.

Evaluating Your Properties and Vehicles

How do you calculate the value of a home or other real estate? While you may need to obtain an appraisal of real estate as part of your divorce process, it is not usually necessary to do so right away. If you and your spouse agree on the value of real estate, you may not need to obtain an appraisal at all. If not, getting an appraisal too early may require you to pay for another if your divorce takes a long time to come to a close. Your attorney should let you know if and when an appraisal is necessary. Prior to the appraisal, you may consult a real estate agent to get a market analysis. This analysis is not as reliable as an appraisal, but it is a good enough starting point when trying to determine the value of a property. You may also check online real estate sites for a general idea as to your home's value. Your town's valuation for tax assessment purposes, if done recently, may also be a good starting point.

What about the value of your vehicles? If a vehicle was recently purchased, determining its value may not be too hard a task. If you are trying to determine the value of a car, there are multiple automobile valuation websites available to help you. In order to get an accurate number, you'll need to know the correct model of your vehicle, any special packages it has, the condition it is in, and its mileage. Your auto mechanic or auto dealer may also be able to give you an idea of your automobile's value.

Pensions

If you have accumulated funds in a pension or some other defined benefit retirement plan that is not in pay status, valuation by you will be difficult at best. Most people leave the value box blank or write "unknown" in it. Follow your attorney's advice, but it is probably a good idea to contact your benefits coordinator and request a plan description and an estimate of your expected monthly benefit. This information may be needed by your attorney in the future.

Ownership of a Business

If you own a business outright or have a financial stake in a business, it is likely that the value of this asset will be difficult to determine. Resist the temptation to write a zero in the value box. It is unlikely that this value is correct. Discuss this matter with your attorney so that you can be as accurate as possible. It may be possible to arrive at a good faith value. If not, you or your spouse may decide to pay a business appraiser to do a business valuation. Whatever you decide to do, it is better to write "unknown at this time" in this section rather than marking it as a zero value or leaving it blank.

Additional Information

There may be places to put additional information on the court form. If there is any financial information that has not been disclosed in the balance of the financial affidavit, discuss it with your attorney. Do you receive money from any other sources? Do you have any other sources of income, even if they are inconsistent or not guaranteed? Are you expecting an inheritance? Are you a party to any other pending court cases that may result in money coming to you or an expense that you may have to pay? Do you have any pending insurance claims? Are you expecting a job change in the near future? Is there any reason why your expenses might change (Did you just move? Did you just incur more debt?). Again, it's best to have all information as accurate as possible and disclose all necessary information as early as possible.

Public Access

It is important to know that your financial affidavit, like the rest of your divorce file, may be accessible to the public. The rules regarding what information may be disclosed to the public and under what circumstances vary from state to state. Some states keep financial disclosure statements sealed (private), allowing them to be accessed only by the parties, their attorneys, any guardian ad litem or attorney for minor children, and the court. Some states seal these documents only so long as the parties have a financial agreement in their divorce matter. In these states, if the case requires any hearings on any disputed financial matters, whether for temporary or final orders or both, then the financial affidavits will be unsealed.

There may be instances in which financial affidavits are always accessible to the public. For privacy concerns, there is certainly an advantage to reaching an agreement if it results in your financial affidavit remaining private. The rest of the documents in your file, however, will likely be publicly accessible regardless of whether you are able to reach an agreement or not.

Keeping Your Financial Affidavit Updated

You will likely complete and review many financial affidavits over the course of your divorce case. While this form requires a good deal of effort to complete initially, it is important that it be frequently updated. Generally, courts do not like to rely on financial affidavits that are many months old. Judges and attorneys want to be sure that any orders or recommendations are based on the most current and correct information. The good news is that updating an affidavit is easier than completing it the first time, as you understand the form better and are simply building on information already provided, not starting from scratch.

TEMPORARY FINANCIAL ORDERS

If you are in need of immediate funds for living expenses or attorney's fees, or if you need to ensure that routine household bills are paid, then your lawyer can put together a temporary agreement with your spouse's lawyer or seek an order from the court to make this happen. Such an agreement or order may be created to answer the following questions:

- How will the mortgage or rent be paid?
- Who will pay for food?

- Who will pay the utility bills?
- Who will pay the daycare bill, insurance bill, or car payment?
- What funds will be used to pay the retainer fee of each spouse's attorney?
- Does one spouse need access to funds or a bank account?
- Does one spouse need to provide the other with a weekly amount of money for personal living expenses?
- Does one spouse need to provide the other with a weekly amount of money for child support?
- Does a college bill need to be paid for a child? What funds will be used for this payment?
- Should any unnecessary services or recurring charges be suspended pending the divorce?

Because many of these expenses are not paid in cash, it is important to identify the way in which they will be paid and make the following decisions:

- Whose checks should be used to pay bills?
- Should certain expenses be charged to a credit card or automatically debited from one spouse's bank account or a joint bank account?
- Should one or both spouses stop using a credit card?

It is important to know how your bills will be paid, and making these financial arrangements as quickly as possible will help you to avoid a good deal of unnecessary stress.

By Agreement

You may discuss these issues with your spouse and report any agreement to your attorneys, or your individual attorneys can discuss and negotiate all these issues. An agreement can be formalized, signed by you and your spouse, and filed with the court. A judge will review the agreement and will likely accept it and make it a temporary order. The terms agreed upon will govern such financial issues while your divorce is pending, and both you and your spouse will need to adhere to this temporary financial order. Keep in mind that a judge is not required to accept an agreement. In the unlikely event that a judge does not accept your agreement, both spouses' attorneys will be advised as to the judge's concern and will need to address it. Occasionally, the terms of an agreement are not formalized and the agreement is not filed with the court, with the parties instead coming to an understanding that each will do what has been promised.

No Agreement

If no agreement can be reached, then a temporary order from the court may be sought. This would also be the case if your spouse was in violation of the automatic orders in regard to finances (e.g., hiding money, incurring unreasonable debt, unreasonably depleting funds or other assets, etc.). A temporary order is initiated by one or both attorneys filing a *motion* with the court. A motion is a document requesting that the court issue a specific order. A motion could ask for one spouse to be ordered to pay support to the other, for one spouse to be ordered to pay certain household expenses, for one spouse to be prevented from further depleting assets, or some other request. A motion must state what the spouse is looking for and why. Different requests require different motions, and it is not uncommon to have several motions filed with the court at one time.

In time, the court will assign a date for a hearing on the motion and you and your spouse will likely be required to appear in court. Your attorney will give you notice and instructions for that day. It is likely your attorney will prepare you in advance for any testimony (sworn statement before the court) you may have to give. Your financial affidavits may be unsealed, as discussed above, and will be a primary consideration in the eyes of the court. In many cases, your attorney and your spouse's attorney will have additional documents or other items they will want to introduce as evidence to the court in support of whatever claims they are making.

After hearing all testimony and comments made by your attorneys, the judge will review the evidence and make a decision. Sometimes a decision on a motion is made at once and you are notified at the time you are in court. More often, the judge takes additional time to consider a motion and issues a decision at a later date. Most temporary orders, in my experience, are issued at the conclusion of a hearing or within one week thereof. Your attorney can tell you what is customary in your area. Unfortunately, there are instances in which judges take much longer than usual and there is normally nothing one can do about it other than wait. Your attorney can let you know if other measures may be taken and when.

Moving Forward Slowly

Unless someone has been treated unfairly in regard to family finances or the household finances have been neglected, usually the best course of action to take is to maintain the status quo in connection with money matters while the divorce is pending—it is typically the least expensive course of action for all to take as well. It's almost always better to spend the time and money necessary to complete your final divorce orders rather than to seek temporary orders, which you will eventually have to replace with final orders anyway. With the help of your attorney, you will have to make this determination based on your situation at the time. Once you and your attorney are satisfied that the basic financial needs of your family are being met, you can focus on what your post-divorce financial orders should look like.

FINANCIAL ANALYSIS

It is important for your attorney, in most cases, to understand the history of your finances during your marriage and be confident of the existing finances prior to recommending a final financial settlement. This requires the accumulation and review of financial documents—many of which were discussed in Chapter 4 on page 43. It also requires the accumulation of other relevant information from both you and your spouse. The process of obtaining and analyzing this information is time consuming, but it is an important part of your attorney's due diligence in representing you.

The Purpose of Analysis

This detailed review should enable your attorney to suggest what financial orders are likely to be made by the judge. Your attorney should also be able to let you know what a best-case scenario and a worst-case scenario would look like, assuming you go to trial. Nevertheless, it is important to remember that no attorney will be able to predict the financial results of your divorce definitively.

As you will see in later chapters, many factors beyond your attorney's control affect how spouses and attorneys negotiate cases, and how judges decide them. A knowledgeable and experienced attorney, however, should be able to provide you with a financial range or property division options you can reasonably rely on. This information will allow you to set some expectations for your case, plan for your post-divorce future, and evaluate settlement offers made by the other party when your attorney starts negotiating.

Waiver of Full Analysis

In some cases, clients wish to waive an in-depth review of the marital finances by an attorney. These people usually feel that they have a good handle on their combined marital income, assets, and debts. They do not have any concerns about prior financial transactions and may have already discussed financial settlement terms with their spouses. If you find yourself in similar circumstances, discuss your reasons for accepting such an arrangement with your attorney and be prepared to sign a document confirming your wishes and absolving your attorney of responsibility for this review not taking place.

Preparing for the Future

It is important to create a budget with your expected post-divorce finances as early as possible. This review of your expected income and expenses will inform you as to what financial steps you should take to make sure you are able to support yourself and your children. Will you need to increase your income or reduce your expenses? Would you like to continue residing in the marital home, if possible, or would you be better off, financially speaking, living somewhere else? Will you be relying on savings, investments, or retirement funds to supplement your income—and is this a sustainable arrangement? Would you be able to pay off a recurring debt, such as a car loan or mortgage, in order to reduce your monthly expenses? What opportunities might you have for additional employment or an increase in earnings? The sooner you get a handle on your post-divorce financial situation, the better. More lead time equates to more choices and a greater chance of financial independence.

The finances of divorcing spouses are often negatively impacted right after the divorce, and for good reason. A divorce, in most cases, doubles the divorcing couple's living expenses and halves their family's previous income. It is very easy to become overwhelmed at the prospect of uncertain or inadequate finances. It may be helpful to consult a financial planner, accountant, or bookkeeper in these matters. It will provide you with a degree of comfort to understand your finances and the steps you may be able to take to improve your financial situation. Your attorney may be able to refer you to one of these professionals.

FINAL FINANCIAL ORDERS

Final financial orders handed down by the court may include child support, post majority educational support, spousal support, and debt and property allocations. The court considers many factors when determining what financial orders it issues. These factors vary from state to state. Relevant evidence needs to be presented by the parties and their attorneys when seeking any financial order from the court. The judge must consider all relevant evidence presented but may decide that some evidence is more important than other evidence.

Parental income and how many children there are to support are the two factors that primarily determine how much weekly child support is to be paid. Disputes between spouses regarding the calculation of child support often arise when one spouse is self-employed, as a self-employed individual may underreport earnings. They may also come up when one spouse is under-earning—i.e., not working at all or not working enough. Your attorney can assist you in proving your income and disproving or confirming your spouse's income if necessary. Relevant factors for spousal support, property distribution, and debt distribution may include:

- length of the marriage;
- ages of the spouses;
- health of the spouses;

- education levels of the spouses;
- future and current earning capacities of the spouses;
- financial needs of the spouses;
- any income-producing assets of the spouses;
- any contribution to or maintenance of assets made by the spouses; or
- contribution to the breakdown of the marriage (also referred to as "fault" for the breakdown of the marriage) by either spouse.

Spouses and their attorneys often have different views on the existence or importance of some of the above factors. Who is deemed at fault for the breakdown of the marriage is typically the most disputed point, followed by the earning capacities of spouses. Disagreement over the contribution that each spouse made or did not make to the accumulation of the combined assets is a close third.

Your attorney will explain which factors are most relevant to your divorce based on the facts of your case and how they might support or work against your claims. From there, you will help your attorney to obtain evidence needed to prove the factors that support your claims and strategize how to minimize the factors that work against your claims.

CHILD SUPPORT

Child support is intended to cover the basic needs of the couple's children, including food, shelter, clothing, school supplies, extracurricular activities, and school field trips. Parents have a legal obligation to support their children. This obligation exists whether the parents were ever married and continues after divorce. With rare exceptions, only children of the couple by birth or adoption are covered. In most states, financial support allocated to children increases as the combined income of the parents increases. This allocated amount will be divided between the parents according to a formula determined by your state. The information that goes into the formula also varies from state to state. This will usually include Parental income, certain allowable deductions (for example, taxes), health insurance costs, the number of children

College Expenses

The law varies from state to state regarding college (or any post-secondary education) expenses of children of divorced parents. In some states, the court may be allowed to make orders requiring one or both parents to contribute to the cost of higher education expenses of their children—regardless of parental agreement on the subject. This may take place at the time of the divorce or at a later date. There will be several factors that the court will need to take into consideration when fashioning these orders. These factors also vary from state to state but will generally include the financial ability of each parent to contribute, any financial contribution the child may be able to make, any savings that has been set aside for higher education, any financial aid that may be available, the cost of the higher education, and other information concerning the school selection process, courses of study, and academic standing of the child. If this type of order is available in your state, your attorney will explain what information will be relevant to the court and how it will be presented so that you may obtain one if you can't reach an agreement with your co-parent.

In some states, a parent cannot be ordered to contribute to this type of expense. If that is the case, a parent can only hope to reach an agreement with the other parent regarding these costs. While a

for which the support is being calculated, and the identification of the custodial parent. In addition to a set weekly or monthly amount that is calculated for basic expenses, a percentage of other expenses, such as unreimbursed medical expenses or work-related childcare expenses, may be ordered to be shared between the parents.

There will normally be few reasons to deviate from the child support number and percentages resulting from the formula. These may include shared custody, earning capacity of a parent (if different from actual earnings), extraordinary visitation expenses of a parent, and extraordinary medical expenses of a parent or child, among others. If any of these deviation criteria exist, then an argument can be made that a different child support number should be ordered. If the parties agree to deviate from the child support amount, or a judge orders a deviation from the court may not be able to make orders of contribution by a parent, these states generally allow the courts to enforce agreements the parents may have reached. If you live in a state that does not allow the family court to make orders in regard to parental contributions to college costs apart from an agreement between the parents, then you need to discuss the pros and cons of trying to negotiate and document a specific agreement for these costs at the time of your divorce. Certainty and having an enforceable order must be balanced with agreeing to a future financial obligation based on incomplete information or a financial ability that may change in the future.

Ideally, regardless of what a judge can and can't order, you and your co-parent will strive to make the best decisions possible with regard to your children's higher education. This will involve frank discussions of financial ability not only with each other, but with your child. Care should be made to agree upon and outline expected financial lay-outs well in advance so that you and your co-parent and your child can plan appropriately. College searches and applications should be consistent with the agreed-upon plan so as to avoid unrealistic expectations or strife. When possible, all parties should be involved in the college selection process. As always, your child's well-being must come first and your child—even if an "adult" at this point—should not be a part of any disagreements.

child support amount, then the specific reasons for this deviation will normally have to be identified. This is to ensure compliance with the guidelines and for future reference by the court if child support needs to be reconsidered.

Who Pays Child Support?

Weekly child support is normally paid to the parent who has primary physical custody of the children by the parent who does not have primary physical custody of them. In shared and split custody situations, total child support due from both parents may be reallocated so that less than the default amount calculated pursuant to the formula used is to be paid from the higher wage earner to the lower wage earner. Sometimes these custody arrangements result in no money exchanges between the parents. This may be especially true if the parents earn similar amounts of money.

For any order that requires a percentage of additional expenses, the payment method may vary, depending on the provider being paid. Few childcare providers or medical or dental providers will agree to divide a bill and accept partial payment from each parent. Most require payment from one parent in full. In such cases, the parent paying the full amount should provide the receipt and proof of payment to the other, and that parent should reimburse the other in the appropriate amount and in a timely manner. Parents should make timely payments directly to those providers who will accommodate shared obligations.

How Is Child Support Paid?

Child support is normally payable on a weekly basis, but some couples agree to biweekly or monthly payments. It is becoming more common to pay child support by way of electronic transfer of funds. This reduces wait time. It also avoids any transfer of money during child exchanges and allows both parties to maintain good records of payments. If a parent does not pay child support on time, the court may order that it be paid by automatic wage execution. This requires forms to be completed by the recipient of child support (or the recipient's attorney) and signed by the court, which are then sent to a state child support enforcement agency. This agency, in turn, sends notice of the court order to the payor's employer, who then has to deduct the child support from the payor's weekly or biweekly wages and send it to the state agency each period. The state agency then sends the funds to the receiver of child support. This option is not available for self-employed individuals or independent contractors.

For How Long Is Child Support Paid?

In a majority of states, weekly child support continues to be paid until the child reaches the age of eighteen, or the age of nineteen if the child is still a full-time high school student. Some states extend child support up to age twenty-one. In cases of mental, physical, or intellectual disability of a child, child support may continue beyond age eighteen or graduation from high school, even if the general obligation ceases at that time.

Since the child support amount is based in large part on the number of children that need to be supported, the number has to be recalculated each time a child ages out. Contrary to popular belief, however, child support does not automatically get reduced to half the amount if one of two children ages out, or to two-thirds the amount if one of three children ages out. Updated financial affidavits and earnings will be used whenever a child is no longer eligible for child support. At this time, child support will need to be recalculated and a new order entered for any remaining children eligible for support.

If your child support order includes an obligation to pay unreimbursed medical expenses, this usually continues until weekly child support ends. It is often the case that parents agree at the time of their divorce to continue to be responsible for this expense, at agreed-upon percentages, after their children age out of weekly child support. This is probably due to the fact that children often continue to be covered by a parent's health insurance policy and are not likely to have the resources available to pay for their own coverage or out of pocket medical or dental expenses. This agreement to pay usually covers the period of time from the divorce until the child is no longer able to be covered under a parent's health insurance policy or obtains their own coverage, whichever occurs first. If payment beyond the child support term is included in your divorce orders, the court can enforce it if a parent fails to abide by the agreement.

Past-Due Child Support

If back weekly child support is owed, either because a child support order is issued retroactively (the duty to pay starts on a date prior to the actual order) or due to nonpayment of court-ordered child support, then the court has to determine how this back amount (sometimes referred to as *arrearage*) is to be paid. It could be paid over time, in that a certain percentage of the total weekly child support is added to the regular payment amount until the arrearage is paid in full. Or the judge may order the arrearage paid in a more timely fashion or even in a lump sum. Regardless, another remedy the court has for nonpayment of support is to make the weekly order subject to an automatic wage execution, as recently discussed. The judge may also order other past due support amounts, such as unreimbursed medical and childcare expenses, to be paid. The payment schedule will depend on the circumstances of each case.

Additional Child Support

Although weekly child support is intended to cover all the basic needs of the children, many parents agree to provide and share in the cost of additional expenses of the children. The amount and types of additional expenses will vary from family to family, depending on the parents' resources and lifestyle. Many agree to divide the cost of agreed-upon extracurricular activities (including gear) or club memberships, some of which can be quite expensive and not feasible based on weekly child support alone. Other additional costs may include those associated with:

- cell phones and other personal electronic devices;
- driver's education courses;
- buying, leasing, or maintaining a vehicle;
- vehicle registration and insurance;
- school parking pass;
- expensive field trips or class trips;
- prom or other special events; or
- high school graduation, SAT prep classes, or college application fees.

If both parents are persuaded to include additional child support in their divorce orders, the types and extent of these costs, as well as the percentage each parent will pay, are discussed and negotiated between the parents (or their attorneys). Any agreement that is included in your divorce orders can be enforced by the court if a parent does not abide by it.

Final Thoughts on Child Support

It's important to remember that child support is for the child, even though it is paid to a parent. It shouldn't be paid grudgingly. Likewise, the parent receiving child support shouldn't complain about financial contributions for the child. The child shouldn't have to hear how much one parent pays the other, that the amount a parent gets is not enough, that the other parent should buy an item for the child because "child support won't cover the cost," etc. Children shouldn't have to worry about how their parents financially support them or be made to feel like a financial burden.

ALIMONY

Alimony, also called spousal support, is a required payment made to an ex-spouse as financial support. Almost all states have a provision in their laws that allow for the possibility that alimony be awarded to a spouse in the absence of agreement by the parties. The purpose of alimony, the factors that are relevant in determining whether or not alimony is awarded, the amount of alimony that must be paid, and the length of time over which alimony must be paid vary from state to state. If ordered, this support may be a weekly, biweekly, or monthly amount that has to be paid for a certain period of time, or it may be an order to pay a lump sum amount. Unlike child support, there are often no specific guidelines or formulas to determine the amount of alimony someone should pay or receive. Instead, spouses can usually negotiate and ask for whatever they think is fair and reasonable, and judges have the authority to order whatever they think is fair and reasonable based on consideration of allowable factors and within any applicable state-prescribed limits. What is "fair and reasonable" is going to depend on the facts of each specific case and the purpose of the alimony. Opinions on the amount of alimony and length of time it should be paid may vary based on who is arguing or deciding a case.

This may not seem very fair at all. It may even be unsettling to be aware that something so important is based on so much subjectivity. These are reasonable and valid concerns, but experienced attorneys and judges have a good idea of how to analyze the factors that the law says must be considered. In fact, they often manage to calculate alimony amounts and terms that are not very different from each other.

Yes, occasionally, there will be a large difference in the arguments presented between attorneys or the opinions of judges. But this usually occurs when unequal importance is placed on certain factors in dispute between the spouses, such as fault for the breakdown of the marriage, earning capacity, etc. Once these facts are aligned or determined by a judge, then this large discrepancy usually goes away. Nevertheless, there is likely not an experienced attorney out there who has not been surprised at one time or another by a judge's ruling on alimony. It is a risk one takes by going to trial, which this book covers in Chapter 8. (See page 113.)

If possible, spouses should try to agree on any alimony terms. If the amount of alimony—or whether someone is entitled to any alimony—cannot be agreed upon, a judge will hear the matter and make a decision at trial. There are two ways alimony may be paid: periodically or in a lump sum. In addition, alimony may be ordered for different reasons.

The Purpose of Alimony

There are generally two main reasons alimony is ordered or otherwise agreed upon. The first is to equalize the household income between the spouses. Marriage is assumed to be a team effort and, unless shown otherwise, each participant should share equally in the household income, assuming other factors, especially the length of the marriage, make this conclusion fair and reasonable. This result most commonly applies in situations in which one spouse earned most, if not all, of the household income during the marriage, while the other spouse typically took on most of the household and childcare responsibilities, although these jobs don't come with a separate income.

It is generally accepted that the spouse who takes on the domestic role is an equal contributor to the household income and finances, as this work has enabled or otherwise supported the other spouse's ability to work outside the home and increase their career opportunities and earning capacity. Alimony in these situations is usually ordered to be made on a weekly or monthly basis and is likely to last a long time—it could be a lifetime or until the recipient remarries—if the marriage was of substantial length and permanent alimony is allowed in the state.

The idea of sharing the income between spouses also applies to situations in which they both work but perhaps one spouse makes significantly more money than the other. The reasons for this disparity will need to be explored, but if a spouse's lower income is due to childcare or some other domestic duty, or by agreement of the parties as a lifestyle choice, and such disparity has continued for a substantial length of time, then it is likely the spouse making more will owe some alimony for some period of time.

Sometimes the factors do not support an equalization of income but some degree of support is deemed fair and reasonable. Perhaps it is determined that a spouse needs a bit of time to get back into the workforce or some training or education to increase their earnings. The purpose of alimony in such cases is rehabilitation, and this alimony is commonly referred to as *rehabilitative alimony*. It is the amount necessary to get back on one's feet, so to speak. This can be agreed upon or ordered to be paid in a lump sum or periodically, over a limited period of time—usually a short one.

Periodic Alimony

Periodic alimony is alimony that is ordered to be paid in regular intervals over the course of time. For example, spouse 1 has to pay $400 a week to spouse 2 over a period of eight years. The amount of weekly support and the length of time such support has to be paid vary from case to case and depend greatly on the factors deemed to be relevant in your state. The purpose of alimony is also a determining factor in each case.

For rehabilitative alimony, the length of time is often tied to whatever it is that the recipient spouse needs to accomplish. It could be tied to the time it takes this spouse to complete a degree or certification. It could be tied to the time it takes this spouse to get back into the workforce. Periodic alimony could be tied to the care of children if the receiver of alimony is providing such care. Perhaps alimony is to continue until a child starts preschool or grade school. Perhaps alimony is to continue until a child graduates from high school. Different family dynamics and resources call for different scenarios. If periodic alimony is based on some equalization of incomes, the length of the marriage is usually a key factor.

As with the amount of alimony, if the period of alimony cannot be agreed upon, a judge will hear the matter and make a decision at trial.

Lump Sum Alimony

Lump sum alimony is, as its name suggests, usually paid in full in one payment. Occasionally, the total amount may be divided into two or three payments. Rehabilitative alimony is sometimes paid in a lump sum. Sometimes periodic alimony is also converted into lump sum alimony, although this is typically an option only for those who have sufficient liquid assets or income from which to pay this lump sum. In these cases, the lump sum is usually less than what the total alimony would be if it were paid periodically over time. This reduction is due to the idea of *present value*—i.e., the idea that money now is worth more than money in the future. It's the same concept behind the vast reduction in winnings a lottery winner must accept when opting for the winnings to be paid in a lump sum instead of in increments over the course of a certain number of years.

The upside of a lump sum payment for the recipient is that the payment is certain and immediate. The upside for the payor is that the payment is certain and over with. In most cases, the lump sum terminates any future alimony support obligation. The payor does not have to worry about future payments or that circumstances in the future may increase the amount required to be paid. Whether or not it is in your best interests to pay or receive a lump sum—and how much of a reduction you should be granted or accept—depends on your circumstances and should be discussed with your attorney.

Most lump sum alimony orders are the result of a negotiated agreement between the parties. But judges may also be able to order lump sums to be paid, sometimes in lieu of periodic or other alimony, and sometimes in addition to periodic or other alimony. Your attorney can provide you with more information on this topic and advise you on whether this option is available and would be suitable in your case.

Lump sum alimony payments are usually due shortly after the divorce has been finalized, but this order may be negotiated between the attorneys or decided by a judge. It may be that certain events have to happen before payment is made, such as the sale of a house or other property. If the amount of lump sum alimony is divided into more than one payment, then the payment timeframe can be negotiated between the attorneys or decided by a judge. This may be the case when the payment is large and there is no immediate availability of funds.

Final Thoughts on Alimony

Alimony is often one of the most disputed issues in divorces. Spouses can spend a good deal of money on attorney's fees to litigate whether a spouse is entitled to alimony and, if so, in what amount and for how long. Given the financial implications of alimony and its effect on both parties, spouses often feel this is money well spent. Going through a divorce can be an emotional rollercoaster. It is important, therefore, to try not to let your emotions cause you to make unwise financial decisions or claims. Let your attorney and anyone who may be hearing your case for settlement purposes (someone from the court or a private mediator) be your guides. They should be evaluating the alimony issue from a purely financial and legal standpoint and will help you to make sound decisions.

PROPERTY AND DEBT ALLOCATION

Sometimes during a divorce, spouses have to decide how property and other assets are to be divided between them and determine how debts are going to be paid and by whom. If they cannot agree or negotiate these things, a judge will decide for them. How assets and debts are ordered to be shared between the parties depends on where the divorce is taking place. There are generally two types of laws: community property laws and equitable distribution laws. States with community property laws generally consider everything accumulated during the marriage as joint. It does not matter much whose name is associated with the property. It does not matter much whose name is associated with the debt. All such property and debt are often divided between the spouses at 50 percent each. These states, however, usually identify specific separate property—even if obtained during the marriage—of which 100 percent will normally be retained by one spouse.

Equitable distribution states don't necessarily carve out separate property. All assets and debts are subject to division between spouses by a court in a divorce matter. This division is based on what the court finds fair and reasonable, given the factors it must consider and the specific facts of the case. It does not matter much whose name is on the title of the property. It does not matter much whose name is associated with a debt. At the outset, all claims regarding all property and debt that exist at the time of the divorce will be considered. This does not mean that the court in equitable distribution states always equally divides property and debts. It may be that the fair and reasonable thing to do is to give one spouse more and one spouse less, depending on the evidence presented at trial.

Separate Property

There are three common categories of separate property. In community property states, these categories are often deemed separate property and usually not divisible between the parties as a matter of law. In equitable distribution states, parties can make claims that all or most of an asset should be deemed separate property and awarded to one spouse over the other. It will be up to the judge to agree or disagree. One category of separate property involves any premarital contribution the spouse may have made. The second involves any inheritance that may have been received by a spouse during the marriage. The third involves any money one spouse may have received during the marriage as a result of a lawsuit or other legal claim. These laws/claims are based on the idea that these categories of property are more appropriately considered individual property, as opposed to marital property, and therefore not subject to division.

Premarital Assets

Premarital assets are money or property a person has prior to marriage. The claim that premarital assets should not be divided is based on the assumption that neither the spouse nor the marriage did anything to contribute to the accumulation of that asset or money. The person making the claim may have to prove the value at the time of the marriage. Any increase in the value of the premarital asset during the marriage may not be considered separate.

Trying to value assets at the time of marriage is often difficult. This is because some assets, like real estate, may not have been valued at the time of marriage. As an example, say someone owns a condominium prior to marriage, and then after marriage the spouses live in the condominium for five years, at which point they sell the condominium and purchase a house. It is unlikely that the spouse who owned the condominium had it appraised at the time of marriage. As such, this spouse would likely only know its value at the time of sale. Other assets such as savings accounts may be difficult to value if records have not been retained and are no longer accessible through their related financial institutions due to age. If documentation does not exist, your attorney may be able recommend other ways to prove your premarital asset value.

A judge has the discretion to agree with this separate property claim or not in equitable distribution states. Generally speaking, the longer the marriage, the less consideration the court will give to this claim. This is especially true if the premarital asset or money has been converted into or merged with a marital asset or funds. And even when this claim is granted, it is very rare to obtain a dollar-for-dollar credit for the premarital contribution. It is more likely that a spouse will get a greater percentage of the present-day value of the asset.

On the other hand, some claims may be made for debts that one spouse may have brought into the marriage that still exist. Perhaps a large student loan still needs to be paid off, or a credit card with a substantial balance is outstanding. The argument would be that whatever debt remains goes to the person who incurred it prior to the marriage. It's a strong argument on its face, but again, the court will hear why this outcome may not be fair given the particular circumstances of the marriage and divorce.

Inheritance

An inheritance received during marriage frequently results in a claim of separate property. The judge will take into account several key factors when considering this claim. Timing is a key factor. An inheritance received soon before a spouse files for divorce is generally going to be a stronger claim as separate property than an inheritance received during the marriage but many years prior to the divorce. How the funds or property were held and used during the marriage are other key factors. Inherited property or funds that were kept in the beneficiary's name alone and not comingled with marital funds or property will generally form a stronger claim as separate property than they would if they were comingled.

Comingling may refer to putting a spouse's name on inherited property or putting inherited funds in an account held jointly with a spouse. Comingling may refer to using marital funds to maintain or improve an inherited property. Comingling may refer to utilizing rental proceeds from inherited property to pay marital bills. There are many more examples of comingling and many other factors the court may consider when determining the division of inherited assets. Your attorney should guide you in pursuing or defending against this separate property claim.

Settlement or Judgment Proceeds

During a marriage, a spouse may have been involved in a legal action against another individual or organization that resulted in the receipt of money from a settlement or judge's decision. If these funds are still around at the time of divorce, the spouse who received them will commonly claim them as separate property. As is the case with inheritances, timing and how these funds were held and used during the marriage will be key considerations in the claim of separate property. But the court will also need to consider why the spouse received these funds. What was the legal claim based on? If the funds were paid for pain and suffering or future medical treatment, then a strong case for separate property could be made. If the funds were paid for lost wages or as reimbursement for expenses, then a strong case for marital property could be made. The particular facts of each divorce case are different. Your attorney will assist you in developing your claim or defense.

CONCLUSION

Compared with all the other matters associated with divorce, issues of property and debt allocation are usually the easiest for spouses to agree upon and accept—even if the agreed-upon terms are not totally to their liking. With the exception of the marital home, which holds some emotional attachment for some spouses, these sorts of items are usually divided without much emotional turmoil. And once it is done, it is done. People can move on. Final financial orders concerning the support of children, payment of the costs of the children's education, and alimony are not often so cut and dried. These may be long-standing orders, and they may need to be modified from time to time or revisited at a later date, reopening old wounds and reigniting past disputes. Furthermore, these orders have the effect of maintaining a financial tie between divorced spouses, which has its own challenges. As always, it's best to be aware of realities such as this so you can prepare for them.

You've been provided with a lot of information thus far, including how to find and hire an attorney, how to prepare for your divorce, how to gather documents to assist your attorney and the court, what you need to know to make decisions regarding your children and your finances, and friendly divorce options. These are all matters in which you will be directly involved. Next, we will discuss some behind-the-scenes events that can directly affect your case, but in which you will not be directly involved, starting with negotiations, moving on to settlement and trial considerations, and concluding with some thoughts on judges.

8.

Negotiation, Settlement, and Trial

The finalization of your divorce will likely occur in stages that include negotiation followed by a settlement or trial. The first stage, *negotiation*, usually involves the attorneys on both sides communicating with each other. The purpose of this communication is to try to reach a mutual agreement on the final terms of the divorce. You will be kept informed of the status of these negotiations and have input through your attorney during this process. If an agreement is reached, then the *settlement* stage will begin. This primarily involves the attorneys drafting paperwork for your and your spouse's review and discussion, and then presenting the finalized, fully executed paperwork to the court. If an agreement cannot be reached, then your case will go to *trial*. This stage entails your attorney presenting your case to the judge for a decision.

The previous chapters have discussed the various steps that must be carried out or considered by you to get to the negotiation stage. As you will see, both you and your spouse will now take a less active role, letting your attorneys move the process toward conclusion. There are, however, ways in which you can still help. It is therefore important to understand what each stage represents and requires.

NEGOTIATION

Negotiation is an attempt by each spouse's attorney to resolve all disputed issues that present themselves over the course of the divorce. Negotiation can be used, if needed, to arrive at a temporary order while the divorce is pending or establish the final terms of the divorce. It involves a back-and-forth exchange of communications, either written or oral, which contain the wishes of the clients and usually reasoning to support their coming to fruition. The reasoning offered may be based on many factors, including legal principles, financial considerations, and emotional persuasions. The process can be very difficult, even for someone who is an expert in the field.

Negotiating a divorce is often more difficult than negotiating other legal matters due to the intensity of emotion involved. The parties to a divorce may have years of history and intimacy together—a fact that changes the playing field for attorneys, as they have to consider this relationship and its effects while conducting their settlement discussions. While you will probably not take part in the actual negotiation of your divorce, knowing about the process can allow you to assist your attorney to obtain the outcome you desire.

Preparation

All the work you and your attorney have done on your case up to this point—along with your attorney's experience, working knowledge of the law, and understanding of how local judges are likely to apply the law—should provide your attorney with sufficient information to adequately conduct settlement discussions with your spouse's attorney. Based on the evidence, your attorney should know the strengths and weaknesses of your claims, and how likely or unlikely it is that your side will prevail at trial on your claims, if a trial is necessary.

By this time, your attorney should also know which claims are most important to you and which claims, if any, you are willing to abandon. If you have not done so already, review with your attorney all the items and terms you are requesting. To avoid any confusion, list your wants in order of importance and share this list with your attorney. It is important for your attorney to know where you will allow for compromise and where you will not during the negotiation period. Usually, the stronger the claim or defense, the harder your attorney will negotiate for it. Weaker claims and defenses are eventually met with compromise or forfeited. Your attorney may still argue a weaker claim without compromise if it is very important to you, but bear in mind that success in this claim might cost you in regard to other claims. Discuss the possible trade-offs involved in fighting for a weaker claim with your attorney so that you may offer your input in the matter.

Risk Tolerance

Prior to negotiation, you and your attorney should discuss how you feel about the possibility of going to trial. The whole point of negotiation is to try to avoid trial—that is, to try to reach an agreement between you and your spouse known as a settlement. If a settlement is reached, a trial becomes unnecessary.

Risk tolerance levels vary from person to person. Those who are less comfortable with risk are referred to as "risk-averse." These people are usually willing to give up more of what they want to avoid the uncertainties of a trial. Those who are more comfortable with risk are referred to as "risk-tolerant." These people are usually willing to take their chances at trial rather than accept something they think is less than ideal. In order to take the right approach in negotiation, your attorney needs to have a good idea of your risk tolerance level.

Underlying Considerations

Most people think that divorce negotiation is all about the bottom line—that is, what is eventually agreed to, such as the parenting plan, division of property, amount of alimony to be paid, etc. In my experience, this is not often true. Spouses may have other interests that take precedence over the bottom line, such as wanting to complete the divorce as soon as possible or not wanting to spend too much money on the process. Emotional considerations such as anger or guilt may also be a driving factor. An attorney's interests may also be about something other than the bottom line, including their appearance in the eyes of their client, how they are perceived by the court, and the amount of money their client has to spend on representation.

The presence of these interests can be strong motivation for a spouse or attorney to act in a certain way during negotiations. Some attorneys try to identify what may be motivating the opposing spouse or attorney and negotiate in such a way as to trigger or satisfy those interests to their client's benefit. Sometimes all it takes for a spouse's need to be satisfied is the opposing attorney's choice of words, acknowledgment of a past wrong, or allowance of the spouse to "win" on some things that may not mean that much to the other party. Sometimes a need of an attorney can be met by allowing unsubstantial changes to the written agreement.

Addressing these needs may be the difference between reaching a settlement and going to trial.

Let your attorney know of any underlying interests your spouse may have. It is also usually helpful for your attorney to know how your spouse handles disputes in general. Does your spouse take a hard-line approach in negotiation, shy away from conflict, or make empty threats? Does your spouse avoid making difficult decisions or waffle immediately after making a choice? The more your attorney knows, the better prepared they will be.

The Negotiation Process

The negotiation process usually starts with one spouse's attorney sending a letter outlining the basic parenting or financial settlement terms being sought to the other spouse's attorney. This letter is known as a *settlement proposal*. It does not matter who initiates this process. The attorney receiving the settlement proposal analyzes it, discusses it with their client, and determines how best to respond. The response may be written or communicated over the phone. Attorneys may also meet to discuss settlement in person, however, in my experience, this is rare in practice. From there, the attorneys will advocate for their clients, emphasizing the strengths of their cases and minimizing any weaknesses. Different attorneys may use different tactics during this process.

Attorney Behavior

Some attorneys are more aggressive than others, no matter the strength of a case or the motivation of a client. These attorneys may take a bold, almost unreasonable, stance at the start, knowing they will need to walk back some of their demands during negotiation. Others may warn of messy or expensive litigation if a settlement is not reached on their terms, threatening to call in friends, family members, or coworkers to testify against the other spouse, or to include testimony that reveals private or embarrassing facts in connection with the marriage or the other spouse. Some negotiate by not really negotiating; they offer a proposal but do not engage in back-and-forth discussion—giving the other spouse's attorney the legal equivalent of the "silent treatment." The goal in this case is to make the other spouse or attorney anxious by not being responsive, perhaps getting them to rethink or change their claims.

There are attorneys who try to bully other attorneys. They make their claims out to be better than they really are and insist that the opposing party will lose if the case proceeds to trial. This approach can be unnerving to a lot of spouses, and even to some attorneys, which is precisely why it is utilized. Besides that, some clients simply like their attorneys to take this type of stance and may have made a point of finding representation that displayed this attitude.

Other attorneys take a softer approach. These attorneys are more likely to start negotiations closer to their final, or "bottom line," terms but may not be as willing to compromise much throughout the process. They engage in dialogue with the other spouse's attorney and are willing to respectfully listen and debate their legal positions. While the attorneys are still advocating for their clients, their negotiation tactics are more nuanced. Their maneuvers may change, depending on the case and, in particular, the underlying motivating factors of the other attorney or spouse.

Regardless of their method, the attorneys will continue to try to reach an agreement on all the terms of your divorce. Your attorney will keep you apprised of the progress and give you the opportunity to weigh in when necessary. You should always have the final say on whether to accept or reject any final negotiated terms. Sometimes that's all that is needed, and an agreement is reached without anyone else's involvement. Other times, more assistance to get to a settlement is required, generally in the form of a neutral third-party opinion on which terms are fair and reasonable or in the best interests of the children.

Independent Third Parties

An independent third party can be someone from the court who is assigned, free of charge, to help in reaching a settlement. This person could be a judge in a pretrial or an experienced private attorney who does volunteer work for the court. Alternatively, a third party may be hired by the attorneys on your case at a cost to you and your spouse. This person can be a private attorney or a retired judge who has reentered the legal field in a private practice.

In any of these scenarios, the facts of your case and the arguments regarding any disputed matters are informally heard by the third party (or parties, as there are usually two—one male and one female—in a proceeding). This usually takes place in a conference room or office where the attorneys each make their arguments. Sometimes clients are allowed to be present and sometimes they are not, depending on the type of proceeding. Following the presentation by the attorneys, the third party or parties consider and discuss the matter and then offer their recommendations for a settlement. If conducted through the court system, this process usually takes about an hour but could go longer if you have an available judge who is making progress with the attorneys. If conducted privately, this process can take several hours to a full day. This input from an unbiased person—especially if it is a judge or a retired judge—is usually highly regarded by both the attorneys and the spouses, and often leads to a settlement.

Your Role

For a lucky few, reaching a settlement is quick and painless. For many, however, it involves a good deal of emotional pain and anguish—the very factors that some attorneys try to use to their client's advantage. Nevertheless, remember the fact that knowledge is power. The more you understand the process, the better prepared you will be, and the greater your chance will be of working out a settlement. You can be of assistance to your attorney by being clear about your wants and needs, identifying those claims that are most important to you, being realistic in regard to any obstacles your case faces, and being candid about your feelings on going to trial and providing relevant information about your spouse.

Negotiation is a very important endeavor and doing it effectively can be the difference between coming to an agreement and having a judge decide the outcome of your divorce. Not all cases will settle, even in optimal conditions, but you want to give the process the best chance to succeed.

The Benefits of Agreement

Putting in the work to come to an agreement is almost always the best path to take in a divorce. The benefits of reaching a settlement are numerous and significant.

Speed and Cost

Settlement negotiation generally starts once discovery is complete but

NEGOTIATION, SETTLEMENT, AND TRIAL

long before a trial date. As such, negotiating a settlement can bring an end to a divorce sooner than proceeding to trial.

Certainty and Control

Negotiating a settlement allows you to know the terms you are being asked to accept and gives you time to consider them. Even if you are not 100-percent happy with all the terms of your divorce settlement, you can control whether or not to accept them.

Privacy

While your settlement agreement, and thus the terms of your divorce, will likely be available to the public, this option spares you from having to testify. As such, all your private thoughts and information regarding the breakdown of your marriage, the care of your children, and your family finances can remain private. In addition, as previously discussed, your financial affidavit may remain sealed and unavailable to the public if you can avoid a trial stemming from disputed financial issues.

Compliance with Orders

Some people are more apt to follow orders if they are the result of an agreement as opposed to the result of a trial. A favorable trial decision loses its flair fast if the "winner" has to chase the other party to comply by returning to court with a contempt motion (i.e., a request of the court to find the opposing party noncompliant, enforce its orders, and issue some sort of punishment to the opposing party, such as a fine, payment of attorney's fees, or incarceration). If you suspect compliance may be an issue in the future, settlement may be the best option in your case.

Shielding Your Children

As discussed in Chapter 6, if custody of your children is in dispute, your children could become involved in the legal process, with the court appointing someone to represent them or advise the court in regard to their best interests. I am aware that a significant motivating factor for the settlement of custodial issues for some parents is to avoid this possibility. It's not that they do not trust the system (although this may also be a concern), but rather that they want to spare their children from having to become involved in the legal proceedings, which is completely understandable.

The Downside to Agreement

Assuming there is an opportunity to reach a reasonable agreement, there is really only one possible disadvantage to settling that comes to mind, which is that it eliminates the need for your attorney to present your case, thus preventing a judge from determining if your spouse has acted wrongly and what the consequences of these actions should be. You don't get to testify and tell your story. This aspect of settling can be disappointing to some.

SETTLEMENT

If both parties come to an agreement on the major terms of their divorce, the fine tuning can begin. One of the attorneys—it doesn't matter which—prepares a draft of the final written agreement, referred to as a *separation agreement*. Included in the separation agreement will be all the major terms, as well as a lot of other language you likely did not discuss with your attorney. Don't worry. Most of the additional language will consist of legal boilerplate items—things that apply equally to you and your spouse and are beneficial to both of you, and language that must be included by law. But there will be other details that will need to be discussed and negotiated in order to complete or complement the major terms.

If your attorney is responsible for drafting the document, then these additional terms should be explained to you before the draft goes to opposing counsel. You should be given an opportunity to ask questions and offer input if necessary. If your spouse's attorney drafts the agreement, your attorney should discuss the additional items with you after reviewing the document so you can decide whether to request any changes or additions. Once all the language has been reviewed, re-reviewed, and approved, you and your spouse will sign the separation agreement along with the other paperwork required to finalize your divorce. You and your spouse will most likely have to update your financial affidavits at this time.

In states that allow a waiver of court appearance when a settlement is reached, neither the spouses nor their attorneys will have to go to court. Instead, the paperwork will be filed with the court electronically. The agreement and other paperwork will be reviewed by a judge and, assuming all is in order, approved—often within a short period of time.

NEGOTIATION, SETTLEMENT, AND TRIAL

This approval means that the court grants your divorce in accordance with the terms you and your spouse have agreed upon and those terms become the final orders of the court.

In the event that the court has any concerns or needs additional information, your attorney will be notified. Either additional paperwork will need to be filed or you will be assigned a day to appear in court. Your attorney will prepare you for this appearance if it is required. In all likelihood, these scenarios won't mean you'll have to go to trial. They will simply mean that the court needs more information, or your agreement needs to be clarified or changed to some extent before being approved.

If you are required to appear in court as opposed to submitting paperwork electronically, the review and approval will take place in the courtroom with you and your attorney present. Any questions the court may have will be asked at that time.

Settle Or Go to Trial?

A lot of thought should be put into the decision to settle your case by agreement or have it heard in court and decided by a judge. A case that resolves by settlement is usually the result of back-and-forth negotiation between the attorneys. During this time, they have, with input from their clients, offered and argued for the final terms of all the parenting and financial orders that need to be made at the time of divorce. The process typically ends with both spouses probably feeling as though they have conceded too much and deserve more but can accept and live with the terms. It is important to remember, of course, that being able to accept the terms is not the same as being happy with them. It is often said that you know you have reached a fair settlement when both sides feel equally cheated. This idea doesn't offer much consolation, but it is often true. If one or both spouses cannot live with the terms, however, then there can be no settlement and your case will head to trial. Trial may also be sought for reasons other than an inability to settle. As with much in life, there are pros and cons to each option.

TRIAL

Most spouses go to trial to finalize a divorce because they have to, not because they choose to. In most cases, they were not able to reach an acceptable agreement. It could be that one or both spouses had terms they were not willing to compromise on, or not willing to compromise on to the extent requested by the other party. It could that one spouse was not willing to participate in the negotiation process or any other part of the divorce proceedings. Such cases require a judge to hear both sides of the story and decide what kind of financial arrangement would be fair and what type of custodial arrangement would be in the best interests of the children. They also require an order stating that the marriage has been dissolved and the spouses are officially divorced.

The Downsides of Going to Trial

Although it may be necessary, going to trial is almost never a good thing. You will likely hear this said throughout your case—from your attorney, a third party assigned to assist you in reaching an agreement, and any judges you may come in contact with during the course of your case. Whether you want to go to trial or not, you need to be prepared for the realities of relying on the court to determine the terms of your divorce.

Cost

The amount of work an attorney has to do to prepare for trial is extensive and, as a result, may be costly. Beyond preparation, it is not unusual for a trial to take several full days to complete. This additional time and therefore expense must be factored in when weighing the decision to go to trial.

Delays

Many clients face their trial day with apprehension but also a measure of relief that the process is finally coming to an end. It is disheartening to say the least, then, when spouses show up in court only to be told to come back another day. It is all too common for courts to schedule multiple trials on the same day, expecting some to settle. When reality ends up not meeting expectations, the courts may not have enough

NEGOTIATION, SETTLEMENT, AND TRIAL

judges to hear every case, forcing them to send some away to be heard at a later date. This delay often means additional legal work will need to be done, and thus more money will have to be spent by the divorcing spouses. Attorneys will need to re-prepare for the new date, which is often weeks, if not months, away. It is a very frustrating issue for all involved.

Testifying and the Public Record

If your case goes to trial, you and your spouse will have to testify. Taking the stand is daunting for many. The anticipation of taking the stand tends to cause spouses to lose sleep and their appetites days before trial. Some even experience health issues. It is not uncommon for any embarrassing information or hurtful feelings that you may have held back to come out on the day of the trial. Testimony can burn bridges not only between you and your spouse, but also between you and your spouse's family. Moreover, most divorce trials are open to the public and transcripts of your trial's testimony may be available to anyone willing to pay for them, including your adult children.

Risk

People going through litigation are necessarily biased and often think there is only one possible fair outcome to a trial—that outcome being a decision in their favor. They expect "justice" to be done. A difficult part of an attorney's job is to get a client to understand and acknowledge that laws and their application can be interpreted differently from judge to judge and thus there is always an element of risk in taking a dispute to trial. Judges can and do differ in their opinions, making predicting the outcome of a legal dispute a difficult task. All experienced trial attorneys evaluate the risk of going to trial. Your attorney should share this risk assessment with you so you can decide how best to proceed.

Why a Trial May Be Necessary

A trial is never a good thing for a spouse to go through, but it is sometimes a necessary thing. Regardless of all the issues recently listed, there are some spouses that want to go to trial for personal reasons. They may feel strongly about telling their story. They may think that testifying will be a liberating experience, especially if they felt controlled or abused by their spouses during their marriage. They may feel strongly about having their spouse admit or explain their actions or inactions. You may be one of these people. While they certainly care about the outcome of the trial, their motivation is not to avoid risk or cost. For them, any "reasonable settlement" that denies them their day in court is unacceptable. Going to court is their way of receiving "justice." If you include yourself in this category of people, it is important for you and your attorney to discuss and recognize this fact right from the start, and for you to acknowledge and accept the risks of going to trial.

Another reason that going to trial may be necessary is that sometimes it is the only way to terminate a marriage. Some spouses refuse to negotiate a divorce settlement. Others are so unreasonable that the terms they propose cannot be accepted. Some people drag out divorce cases to punish their spouse, others to delay the inevitable divorce and possible obligations that may come with divorce orders. In situations such as these, trial is the only solution, as no one can force a spouse to be reasonable or agree to any particular settlement terms.

The Trial Process

In most cases, your trial date is provided early on in your case, along with other court dates you may or may not require. This is the court's way of being proactive. Since it takes a long time to secure a date for any hearing due to the volume of cases, the court assigns dates early on. This gives spouses plenty of time to conduct discovery and negotiate, while also letting them know when they will need to be ready for trial should one be necessary. Having trial dates set in advance tends to mitigate conflict with dates and prevent cases from lingering too long in the system, which is important to the court.

You and your attorney will need to be ready as your trial date approaches. It is likely that you have watched trials on television or in movies, but it is quite a different experience to be one of the parties involved in a divorce trial. You will be sitting in a courtroom next to your attorney, watching a judge preside over your case. Despite all the time and effort you may have put in with your attorney to get to this point, the trial itself can still be very nerve-racking. Nevertheless, the more you know about going to trial, the fewer surprises you are likely to face.

Attorney Preparation

There is a tremendous amount of preparation to do to be ready to try a case. Ideally, your attorney has been preparing for trial since the beginning of your case, gathering evidence to support your claims or defend against your spouse's claims should the need arise. Nevertheless, once your attorney is certain of your going to trial, there will still be a lot of work to do. The exact steps will vary from attorney to attorney, but the overall process is essentially the same. All the information that has been gathered has to be broken down, reorganized, and reviewed to ensure that nothing is missing. The *proposed orders*—the terms you would like the judge to order—and the *closing argument*—your reasoning behind why these terms should be ordered—need to be prepared. Your attorney must also analyze each element of your claims (and defenses) and verify the evidence that supports these claims (and defenses).

Once all the evidence has been organized, it must be prepared for trial. Sensitive information such as birth dates, social security numbers, and account numbers must be removed from any documents that are going to be filed with the court. Each piece of evidence needs to be labeled and multiple copies (for the court, the opposing party, and the client) need to be made. A complete copy, along with other paperwork, has to be submitted to opposing counsel and the court prior to your trial date. Attorneys need to provide the court and opposing counsel with notice of their proposed orders and the evidence they intend to file with the court, and a list of witnesses they intend to call. Your attorney will also have to work with you and any of your witnesses on testimony. At minimum, your attorney will need to prepare a list of questions to be asked in connection with the documents being entered into evidence. Your attorney also has to try to anticipate the questions you and your witnesses may be asked by opposing counsel, and how you and your witnesses will respond.

Finally, a good attorney will work to perfect a closing statement, anticipating and preparing possible responses to any concerns the judge may raise as well as any objections made by opposing counsel, preparing objections to evidence offered by opposing counsel, and going over all aspects of the trial until they have been committed to memory. It is a lot of work, but it is your best shot at a positive outcome if your case is going to be heard by a judge.

Client and Witness Preparation

Your attorney will need to prepare you and your witnesses for trial. This will likely involve a "dry run" through the questions and evidence your attorney intends to present. This is intended to let you and your witnesses know what to expect, make sure the questions elicit the expected responses, and correct any mistakes or omissions in your attorney's questions. This usually takes place at the attorney's office but may also be conducted by phone or video conferencing. Each witness, including you, will be prepared individually. In addition to the questions your attorney plans on asking of you and your witnesses, it is likely that the practice will include questions that may be asked by opposing counsel. If you are not sure how to answer a question, your attorney can give you guidance.

Although it is extremely important and required that you answer all questions as honestly and accurately as possible, there may be a preferred way of responding to certain questions. In addition to reviewing your testimony, your attorney will likely go over the evidence, witnesses, and proposed orders of your spouse. Finally, your attorney should tell you what to expect by way of court procedure during a trial.

Arbitration

Arbitration is an alternative dispute resolution process for contested divorces that need to be presented to and decided by a decision maker. This process is private and replaces a trial. Instead of having a case heard in court by a judge, the case is presented to an arbitrator in an office or conference room. An arbitrator is someone who has been trained in adjudicating matters and is agreed upon by both parties' attorneys. This person is often a retired judge but may also be an experienced family law attorney. The business of getting a divorce matter arbitrated varies from state to state. Some states do not allow divorces to be arbitrated at all, while some may limit the types of issues that an arbitrator can hear and decide upon. Benefits of arbitration include privacy (the proceeding is

NEGOTIATION, SETTLEMENT, AND TRIAL

Your Day in Court

On the appointed day, you will likely meet your attorney at the courthouse early. You may have to take a day off work or arrange for childcare. After finding parking and going through the courthouse's metal detectors and marshal station you will be directed to the appropriate floor and courtroom. You and your attorney may go over some last-minute details, or your attorney may need to talk to your spouse's attorney or the court prior to the start of your case.

You and your attorney will then enter the courtroom, sit at a table, and await the appearance of the judge. The judge will call your case and direct the clerk to swear in the parties. You will be asked to stand, raise your right hand, and swear to tell the truth during the proceedings, as well as provide your name and address for the court record, as will your spouse. After any preliminary matters that may need to be discussed between the attorneys and the judge have been addressed, the plaintiff's attorney, who almost always goes first, will be asked to call their first witness. This is usually you or your spouse, although it may be a third party. When you are called to testify, you will need to leave the table you are sitting at and take a seat next to the judge, commonly referred to as

---

not open to the public and often no transcript of the proceedings is made), control (the attorneys can choose an arbitrator and the days and times of the hearing, and can often decide upon other variables, such as how the case will be presented and whether the parties will strictly adhere to the rules of evidence or follow a more relaxed presentation), and avoidance of delays. A downside is that the opportunity to appeal or otherwise challenge the decision of the arbitrator is very limited compared with going to trial. (There is also the cost involved, which is the responsibility of the divorcing spouses.) Once an arbitrator's orders are filed and accepted by the court, they can be enforced like any other orders. If you think you may be interested in arbitration, you can discuss it in more detail with your attorney to see if it is available and whether it might be a good option in your case.

Judges Are People, Too

What do you think of when you hear the word "judge"? Many think of an older man who is wise. Some think of a stern woman, someone like Judge Judy, who is not afraid to call people out. Either way, the expectation is that the judge is going to give the case their full attention and act fairly and correctly. And this is what happens most of the time. Occasionally, it doesn't. Judges have an incredibly difficult and demanding job, and sometimes they're not always at their best. Most judges consistently do a good job and take their responsibilities seriously, but they are still human. They get tired, sick, irritable, and distracted just like the rest of us. Sometimes they are simply overworked.

Over the years, I've come to learn that some judges who heard my cases on certain days were preoccupied with various life issues, spanning from the serious (having a parent in hospice) to the frivolous (obtaining a Christmas present during their lunch break). I had no knowledge of what was going on in the minds of these judges when I was arguing my clients' cases. As an attorney, I can only hope that they were able to put their cares aside and give my clients' cases their full attention. I know, however, that this is not

"taking the stand." You will likely not be allowed to take anything with you, especially any notes.

From this point on, the attorneys will call witnesses and ask them questions in a particular order. During this examination they will also introduce or refer to documents in evidence. When an attorney calls a witness to the stand for questioning, it is known as *direct examination*. After direct examination, the opposing attorney may also question this witness. This is known as *cross-examination*. When the attorneys are done questioning the witnesses and presenting other kinds of evidence, they rest their cases. At this time, the judge usually allows the attorneys to make brief closing arguments. A closing argument should be a summary of the orders being sought from the judge and how the evidence presented supports the client's claims or refutes the claims of opposing

NEGOTIATION, SETTLEMENT, AND TRIAL

always possible, and that judges may not always perform to the best of their abilities.

Besides the risk of a good judge having a bad day, there is also the risk of getting a judge who may not be preferred due to other concerns. Although rare, sometimes people encounter judges who may be inconsistent in their application of the law, or prone to making legal mistakes. Some judges are too soft, never holding anyone accountable for anything. There are judges who seem to try their best not to make a decision, constantly putting the disputed issues back on the parties or the attorneys for resolution. There are judges who may be too strict, choosing form over function. There are judges that proceed too quickly, perhaps not giving each side the appropriate time to present their case or fully understand what is happening. And there are judges who often delay matters or make them worse by introducing issues about which neither party has complained. Being assigned any of these types of judges presents additional challenges for the attorneys involved in a case.

Attorneys do not get to choose which judge hears their cases. It is important to know that this is part of the inherent risk of going to trial.

counsel. This usually concludes the trial. Some cases take less than a day and some cases take several days to complete.

The judge will then need to make a decision. Some judges make their decisions from the *bench*—where the judge sits in the courtroom—at the conclusion of a trial. This is done orally and then put in writing and sent to the attorneys at a later time. Most judges tell the parties and attorneys that they will consider all they have heard and issue a written decision shortly thereafter. Occasionally, a judge may require additional information concerning a claim's legal basis or an interpretation of how the law applies to the facts of a particular case. In such instances, the attorneys may have to prepare and file written legal support for their positions, known as a *brief,* and will be given reasonable time to do so. The time allowed for a judge to render a decision in a case depends on the state in which the case is located and can last many months. In my experience, most written decisions are received within two to four weeks from the last day of trial or the day any briefs are due.

Due to the uncertainty associated with a trial, if there is a reasonable settlement option on the table, most attorneys will recommend you take it. Most trial attorneys are not afraid of trial and actually enjoy the process from a professional standpoint. They do, however, recognize the significant financial and emotional aspects of going to trial, in addition to the risk of receiving an unfavorable decision. Neither you nor your attorney should ever take going to trial lightly.

CONCLUSION

Negotiation is the beginning of the end of your divorce process. It is very important, regardless of the outcome. If successful, it results in a settlement of your case, with all the terms of your divorce agreed upon by you and your spouse. If unsuccessful, it leads to a trial but has also further prepared you and your attorney for what to expect and how best to present your case. It is common for emotions to run strong as your case nears its resolution. For some people, the conclusion is bittersweet. They welcome the end of the process but mourn the end of the marriage. Others may dwell on the causes of the breakdown of the marriage, which are often brought to the forefront during this time.

It may be difficult to remain focused or even completely understand the legalities involved with the negotiation, settlement, and trial processes. Your attorney should be able to offer you plenty of advice during this stage. It is usually best to listen to your attorney and strongly consider all information presented by your attorney and any third party assisting in your case. They are all there to help you.

9.

Abuse, Addiction, and Mental Illness

Among the many factors that can lead to the breakdown of a marriage, there are three that I refer to as "red flag" issues: spousal abuse, addiction, and mental illness. In some cases, these difficult and often destructive problems have been affecting the marriage for a short time. In other cases, they have been there for years. At a certain point, the burden, frustration, fear, and disappointment that result from these issues lead a spouse to consider divorce. You may have reached this point. If that's how you find yourself, I think it important to provide you with some basic information and an assurance that these problems can and will be dealt with within your divorce process.

The presence of any of these circumstances in your divorce means that there is a lot more work to be done for all the parties involved—you, your spouse, the attorneys, and the court. The consequences of these afflictions can be wide-ranging. Just as they affect both your and your spouse's daily lives, so, too, will they affect the divorce process and become an important consideration when discussing and negotiating many, if not all, of the terms of your divorce. The question is: How are these issues typically handled in a divorce proceeding?

If a case involves any of these issues, safety is the primary concern and the matter to which initial attention is devoted. Once steps are taken to ensure, or at least minimize, the risk of harm to you and your children, attention is then focused on evaluation and treatment. Since most family law attorneys and judges are not often experts in any of these three subjects, they frequently rely on experts in mental health or substance abuse to assist them with such cases.

This chapter discusses these red flag issues in detail and how they can be addressed during your divorce. If you are dealing with any of these issues, it is important to know you are not alone, although you may feel that way. It is likely that you have family or friends to support you. Regardless, there are many people in the court system or associated with community organizations who are ready and willing to assist you. You just have to reach out and ask for help.

ABUSE

Abuse can be physical, emotional, or both. It can occur as a repeated behavior or sporadically. These knowingly hurtful and cruel actions may be aimed at a spouse, a child, or both. This behavior is usually rooted in a desire to control the victim. It is often a learned behavior—quite often the abuser has been abused. Abusiveness can also have a number of other causes, including the misuse of drugs or alcohol, and behavioral disorders.

Physical Abuse

Physical abuse comes in two forms: non-sexual and sexual. Examples of non-sexual physical abuse include choking, hitting, slapping, biting, pinching, and kicking. Sexual abuse refers to any unwanted sexual contact or exposure, including intercourse, oral sex, induced pain, and forced nudity.

Physical abuse often occurs in a repeated pattern. There is usually a period of increasingly threatening behavior (which is a form of abuse on its own) that leads to an actual assault, which is then followed by expressions of guilt and sorrow on the part of the aggressor. Subsequently, the abuser usually goes through a period of acting "normal" or even kind. Victims may start to trust their abusers again and even think they may have overreacted to the abuse. An abuser may also take advantage of a victim's feelings of self-doubt, perpetuating them and causing the victim to feel at fault for the abuser's actions.

All too often, victims make excuses to themselves and others regarding the abuse, or hide the incidents from others, which can lead to feelings of shame when the abuse happens again.

Emotional Abuse

This form of abuse is characterized by attempts to control a person by non-physical, psychologically coercive means. There are many ways in which an abuser may try to do so. An abuser may yell or swear at a victim. An abuser may threaten to harm a victim physically, or someone the victim cares about. An abuser may threaten to harm a victim's pet. An abuser may threaten to divulge information that would humiliate a victim.

In an effort to try to eliminate a victim's sense of autonomy, an abuser may seek to dictate what a victim wears, where a victim goes, and with whom a victim spends time. Emotional abusers often put down their victims, repeatedly telling them they are not smart enough to make their own decisions. They often engage in "psychological warfare," accusing victims of being "crazy" and making them think things didn't happen the way they think they did. Some use finances as a means of control, limiting victims' access to money, credit cards, or even employment, so that they are completely dependent on the abusers.

Whatever the method of emotional abuse, this type of mistreatment occurs frequently and can lead to psychological and physical illness for victims. It is also important to note that those who witness abuse, whether emotional or physical, such as a child who sees one parent being threatened or hit by the other, should be considered victims of abuse themselves.

Getting Help

This cycle of abuse must be broken. If you are reading this book in hopes of getting out of such a situation, it is important that you reach out for help. As a victim, you need to be protected from your abuser. This may involve calling the police, a domestic violence hotline, or other emergency personnel. (See Resources on page 169.) It may involve getting away from an abusive spouse by relocating, whether temporarily or permanently, to a safe location. The path that is most appropriate for a victim will depend on the victim's circumstances.

If you are the victim of an abusive partner and have an attorney, it is imperative that you make this fact known to your attorney. Your attorney will direct you to the appropriate resources and take steps to gain legal protection for you as circumstances allow. This may involve contacting the police, in which case a criminal court may issue orders of protection.

In the case of the arrest of an abusive spouse, it is likely that this individual will be ordered by the criminal court to attend domestic violence counseling or participate in a domestic violence program. Often, temporary divorce orders regarding child custody and access will conform or supplement whatever restrictions are already in place pursuant to the criminal court's orders.

An abused spouse may also seek help from a civil court, even if no criminal charges are filed or pursued. This may include filing for a protective order or filing for an emergency order of custody. If there are minor children involved, a judge can also order a mental health or substance abuse evaluation as well as treatment of the abusive spouse if enough reasonable evidence warrants it. The goal is to reduce the likelihood of a spouse's continued abusive behavior.

Unless there is an agreement or admission from a spouse, a hearing in civil court will likely be necessary to obtain protection, evaluation, or treatment. Evidence that will need to be presented will include testimony. The victim will have an opportunity to explain to the judge what behavior their spouse has exhibited and how it has negatively affected them and their children. Other witnesses to the abusive spouse's behavior may also be called to testify. Evidence may also include relevant hospital or medical records, arrest records, emails, texts, pictures, or videos. The amount of such evidence can differ greatly from case to case. If this situation applies to you, your attorney will help you gather such evidence.

Both victim and abuser will probably need a good deal of therapy or other mental health treatment for a good period of time after the cycle has been broken. It is especially important to monitor an abuser's compliance with mental health treatment or substance abuse treatment recommendations when fashioning custody/parenting plan divorce provisions. Special provisions regarding communication and interaction between victim and abuser will need to be considered as well in order to protect the victim from the possibility of future abuse.

Breaking the Cycle

It takes a lot of courage and support to get out of an abusive relationship. It also takes a lot of courage and support for an abuser to admit to having been abusive and obtain the treatment needed to address the problem. Whether you are a victim or an abuser, you owe it to yourself and your children to get the help you need. Your divorce is an opportunity to take the appropriate steps and obtain the necessary protections to break the cycle of violence and live a better future.

ADDICTION

Addiction is a medical condition in which an individual has an overpowering compulsion to look for and take a specific substance. For people suffering from addiction, cravings for drugs or alcohol can affect their behavior to the exclusion of just about everything else. They may lie or steal to get what they want. Even if they know what they are taking is harmful to their health and the relationships around them, they are powerless to stop without help.

When confronted, people with addictions often try to minimize or hide their behavior. It is often difficult to get those who suffer from addiction into treatment, and relapses are common. Frustration and disappointment are common when dealing with someone with this disease. Below is a brief overview of some of the different types of addiction one can have and how they may be addressed in the context of a divorce.

Substances

Dealing with substance abuse is not easy, even in a strong, healthy relationship. It's nearly impossible when a relationship is struggling. It adds a whole other layer of stress and difficulty for the whole family when a couple is going through a divorce. If you have a spouse with a substance abuse problem, you first have to ask yourself several questions: Is your spouse a danger to him or herself? Is your spouse a danger to you? Is your spouse a danger to your children? There may be different answers to these questions. Each poses different risks and requires different ways to address these risks.

A safety plan that covers all scenarios, to the best of your ability, needs to be discussed with your attorney right away. Professional evaluations should be considered and emergency orders, if needed, should be sought. Such orders may include a spouse's removal from the home, temporary suspension of access to the children, or supervised parenting time with the children.

Alcohol

Drinking alcohol to such a degree that it negatively interferes with any aspect of one's life is problematic. The severity and frequency of this interference can vary from person to person and may progress in certain individuals over time. Some people can misuse alcohol and not be alcohol dependent. Binge drinking, heavy drinking, and drinking and driving are examples of alcohol misuse. A person who misuses alcohol may be driven to make better choices through education, negative consequences, or legal restrictions.

The inability to control one's drinking is alcohol dependency. Alcohol dependency is a medical condition that can develop as a result of the misuse of alcohol over time. A person may even be genetically predisposed to becoming alcohol dependent, although this predisposition is not necessary for someone to become an alcoholic. Those who are dependent usually require intensive treatment in various forms to manage this condition. Treatment may involve enrollment in a rehabilitation program, behavioral therapy, medication, or ongoing support through groups or individuals. There is no cure for alcohol dependency. Becoming alcohol-free is an ongoing process.

Drugs

Drug abuse can refer to both legal and illegal substances. Legal substances include prescription drugs, over-the-counter medication, and cannabis. As with alcohol, misuse of drugs can lead to dependency due to changes in the brain that occur with continuous use. Treatment for drug dependency can be similar to that for alcohol. A big difference for our consideration is the criminal component often involved with drug use—the illegality in obtaining and possessing controlled substances. This aspect is a cause for concern, as it can expose the individual obtaining the drugs to criminal association, police interaction, and arrest. This exposure could, in turn, put the individual's spouse or children at increased risk of emotional or physical harm.

Evaluation, Testing, and Monitoring

Drug and alcohol testing or evaluation is sometimes ordered or agreed to during the course of custody and parenting time disputes. Judges have

ABUSE, ADDICTION, AND MENTAL ILLNESS

an obligation to make decisions that are in the best interests of the child when parental issues are brought to court. Once a valid accusation of substance misuse or dependency has been raised, determining whether there is, in fact, a substance abuse issue at play is consistent with this obligation. As such, a judge can order a parent to submit to testing or attend a substance abuse evaluation whether the parent agrees with the order or not.

Drug and alcohol evaluations are used to determine if someone misuses or is addicted to any substances. The goal is not only to identify or rule out a problem but also to provide an opportunity for education and treatment if necessary. Drug and alcohol evaluations involve meeting with a medical professional. This professional obtains information about the person being evaluated by interviewing them and having them complete answers to a variety of questions. It may include a review of the person's medical and prescription records or talking to family members or other close contacts. The evaluator discusses any areas of concern with the person being evaluated, offers options for treatment if they feel it necessary, and issues a written report containing their assessment results and any recommendations for treatment.

Drug and alcohol testing is used to determine if someone has used certain substances. Testing can be a one-time event, repeated over time, or involve a continuous period of monitoring for substances. Types of one-time and repeated tests include urine tests, hair follicle tests, and breathalyzer tests. A urine test is the most common. A breathalyzer test tests only for alcohol but provides real-time results and is easy to use and cost-effective. A hair follicle test is preferred by most attorneys, since it tests for a wide variety of substances. It can detect substances going back over a longer period of time and is the hardest to manipulate. An alcohol detection bracelet may be worn for continuous monitoring of alcohol consumption. A drug sweat patch may also be worn for continuous monitoring of substance consumption.

It is important to keep in mind what testing can and cannot do. Testing can demonstrate a finite period of sobriety or lack of sobriety. Testing can confirm suspicions or provide assurance. Testing can provide immediate notice of a potentially unsafe situation. Testing cannot absolutely protect children. Testing cannot prevent a parent from engaging in certain behavior. Testing cannot cure a disease. Testing cannot absolutely prove or disprove the presence of a substance abuse issue.

Accepting Testing

Sometimes spouses willingly submit to an evaluation or test because they feel they have nothing to hide and do not think the testing or evaluation is intrusive. Other times they submit to it because they recognize they have a substance abuse problem and need help. This type of cooperation can advance the divorce process more quickly than if such testing is met with objections, which is why many attorneys counsel their clients to agree to testing or evaluation. Agreeing to be tested or evaluated can also allow a spouse (and a spouse's attorney) to have more input on the type of evaluation or testing to be used.

Provisions for the start or extension of parenting time immediately after a negative test can also be discussed and included in an agreement. Regardless of the type of testing chosen, it is important that the agreement be clear as to the specifics of the testing—i.e., when and how the test is to be administered, who will get the results and how, who will pay for the test, what constitutes a failed test, and what immediate steps, if any, will be taken upon notice of a failed or skipped test.

Denying Testing

If a spouse refuses to be tested, then a hearing must be held in front of a judge, who will then make a determination as to whether or not there exists good cause for substance abuse evaluation or testing. Evidence that will need to be presented by a spouse who is seeking to obtain a court order to force the other spouse to undergo some type of testing or evaluation will, of course, include testimony. The spouse seeking the court order will have an opportunity to explain to the judge why there is a problem that may lead to safety concerns in regard to the children. Other witnesses may be called to testify in connection with the accused spouse's substance abuse. The spouse facing the accusation may also testify. (It is not uncommon for a person who is substance dependent to admit to concerning behavior but suggest it's under control.) Evidence may also include relevant hospital or medical records, arrest records, pictures, or videos. Your attorney will help you gather such evidence.

If a judge finds good cause to order an evaluation or testing, it will be the judge, not the spouse requesting it or the attorneys, who will determine the type of evaluation or testing necessary, the testing procedure used, and what will happen in the event of a positive or negative test result. A recommendation for treatment or a positive drug test result can lead to restrictions such as supervised or suspended parenting time or continued substance monitoring. This spouse who has been ordered to test may also be required to attend a recommended substance abuse treatment or program. A negative test result or evaluation can lead to regular contact with children and a decrease or suspension of future testing.

Destructive Behavior

Addiction can refer not only to substance dependency but also destructive behavior. Addiction characterized by destructive behavior can be very intrusive and disruptive to an addict's life and relationships. It involves an uncontrollable urge to engage in activities such as gambling, sex, pornography, internet use, or video games. These behavior-based addictions must be addressed during the divorce process, as they may negatively impact a spouse's ability to supervise or care for children. Such behaviors may also negatively affect the health or employment ability of a spouse and can often lead to a loss of marital assets. As with drug and alcohol addictions, there are methods of evaluation and courses of treatment for those who experience behavior-based addiction. It is important to try to get the affected spouse help and secure immediate protection of the marital finances. Discuss options with your attorney if this situation applies to you.

An Opportunity to Understand

Sometimes a person's addiction is hard to spot. One knows there's something wrong, but that person is able to hide it—for a while. Then again, sometimes addiction is very obvious. Those concerned may try to offer help, but it never seems to work. At a certain point, some spouses realize that divorce may be their only way out. While there is no cure for addiction, recovery is possible. For addicts of any sort, however, recovery depends on their wanting to get better.

While the divorce process will be stressful, it is also an opportunity for addicted spouses to understand what their addictions have done to their families and obtain (or get back into) treatment. Where children are involved, their safety is paramount. Although the goal should never be to shut out a parent from a child's life, obtaining orders that restrict a spouse's access to the children to the extent necessary to ensure their safety is not something about which one should ever feel guilty.

MENTAL ILLNESS

Approximately 20 percent of people in the United States suffer from mental health disorders. Due to the nature of the disease, it can be years before someone is diagnosed let alone treated for an issue. Many with mental health problems refuse treatment or discontinue treatment after

Narcissistic Behavior

There is a specific type of personality that I have found very difficult for my clients to deal with. It is a personality type that tends to create conflict as the process of a divorce unfolds. So, who are these people? They are the highly self-centered individuals commonly called "narcissists." Chances are, however, that they have never been diagnosed as such. These people are selfish, self-absorbed, detached from reality, and incapable of recognizing the damage they inflict. They are everyone's best friend one minute and then nasty to them the next. They appear to lack empathy. They love to hear themselves talk, convince themselves that they are solely responsible for every good idea or fortune, and never accept any blame or responsibility when things go wrong. In short, they think they are doing the world a favor by waking up each day. Whether or not they suffer from a personality disorder in earnest, these people are very difficult to relate to in the best of circumstances. And going through a divorce with a narcissist can feel like an insurmountable problem.

You have to play by different rules to minimize the manipulation when going through a divorce with a narcissist. Narcissists should be given set choices, not open-ended options. They should not be allowed to rewrite history but only to talk about the future. They must be kept on topic. They must be told what specific steps they are to take and what proof of those steps having been taken will be expected, and then they must be held accountable to these starting. All of this can lead to ongoing challenges when it comes to keeping a relationship on track and addressing parental responsibilities. Unfortunately, mental illness can worsen when stress and other complications of divorce are involved.

If your spouse's mental health impairment is a threat to your safety or the safety of your child—or even to your spouse—it needs to be addressed. Extreme situations may require the safety plans and court intervention outlined in the abuse section earlier. It may be advisable to request a court-ordered psychological evaluation. In other cases, evaluation or a return to treatment may be agreed upon. Divorcing

---

dictates. There must be agreed-upon consequences of noncompliance. Both parties must stick to the written agreements and orders, and these agreements and orders should be clearly stated and contain no wiggle room.

When dealing with a person with narcissistic tendencies, you must minimize the chance of chaos because it is in chaos that such a personality thrives. Do not take the bait and engage in any sort of argument. Yes, this is easier said than done, but it is possible. Forget about coming to a fair deal in a reasonable amount of time. Forget about anything with the word "reasonable" in it. Don't invest much time in negotiation. Simply bear down and go through the legal process. Expect to deal with delays and claims of confusion or misunderstanding. Expect complaints that claim you are the unreasonable one. Expect a backlash when a narcissist's back is against the wall.

I am not a mental health professional, but I've come to believe that many people with this type of personality can't help themselves. They are unable to be observant or objective about their own behavior. My years of experience in dealing with people who have these tendencies in court has led me to know that chances are high that they will continue to act the way they do, even if they are held accountable by the court for their behavior. They will just view it as another wrong done to them. As such, if your spouse happens to have these tendencies, you would do better to spend your time and money on professionals who can teach you and your children coping strategies rather than on efforts to change this person.

spouses have the opportunity to address such concerns and try to reach such agreements with the mental health professionals provided by the court.

There are many different types of mental illness. The severity of a mental health disorder may vary from person to person, as may the success of treatment. Some mental illnesses cause symptoms that obviously affect the person afflicted, such as depression, eating disorders, and schizophrenia. It is easy to sympathize with people who suffer from these conditions and not take personally any inconvenience they may cause. Other mental illnesses are harder to recognize and can frustrate those who have to interact with an afflicted individual. It can seem like the person afflicted is acting difficult on purpose. Furthermore, it can appear as though the person afflicted does not care about the offense or disruption they've caused. This is often the case with personality disorders such as narcissism. (See inset on page 140.)

It is hard to be supportive when someone behaves in such a way that causes you frustration, anxiety, or worse, but it is worth considering that this person may not wish to cause you or your children any harm. Of course, most people want to have healthy relationships and be good parents. If you have a spouse with a possible mental illness who is open to discussing it with a qualified therapist, it may be worth the trouble to do all you can to be supportive. If progress can be made, it may save you and your children from years of difficulty and hurt feelings. It also may be a good idea to seek some therapy for yourself and your children. In addition to addressing the personal feelings and effects of having a spouse with mental illness, there are coping skills that can be learned to help manage difficult relationships.

Once treatment of the afflicted spouse has been obtained, ways of encouraging and monitoring compliance will often need to be considered by attorneys and the court when fashioning any temporary or final divorce terms that include child custody or parenting plans. The goal is to get the affected spouse to function at the best possible level they can. This will enable them to get through the divorce process, be a responsible and reliable parent, and hopefully make the process easier for their spouse.

In the event that treatment is refused or not complied with, then additional protective measures will need to be considered by the attorneys

ABUSE, ADDICTION, AND MENTAL ILLNESS

and the court. These may consist of supervised parenting time, loss of legal custody (the right to make decisions for your children), or other restrictions deemed necessary to protect the children and other spouse.

CONCLUSION

It is not uncommon for divorcing spouses to accuse each other of being abusive or mentally unstable, especially when custody or parenting plans are in dispute. Care must be taken to list concerns on a good faith basis or you could lose credibility with the court. If there are serious concerns regarding abuse, addiction, or mental illness, there are ways to address them. The process is rarely easy, and setbacks are to be expected, but it is worth the trouble to secure safety for yourself and your kids and obtain treatment for your spouse. The bottom line is simple: In such situations, in order to turn your life around, you have to make a decision to stand up for yourself—and your children, if any. As you will see in the next chapter, getting ready for life after divorce is as important as preparing for the divorce itself.

10.

Life after Divorce

This chapter is about the future—your future. Perhaps you have not yet started the divorce process or are in the middle of one. Either way, you are likely going through a difficult time. Looking ahead, the hope is that once your divorce has been granted, you will be in a better place. The end of your marriage, however, does not necessarily mean the end of your relationship with your ex-spouse. Some divorced spouses are able to walk away from their marriage without any further connection to one another, but most are not. Having children or ongoing financial obligations with your ex-spouse means the lines of communication between you both will need to be maintained. It is important to be aware of what may come up as you navigate this new type of relationship with your former spouse. You can prepare for and even embrace your post-divorce life.

THE LINGERING REALITIES OF DIVORCE

Once your divorce has been finalized, you'll have to face your future with a few things in mind. If children are involved in the divorce, you will most certainly still have to associate with your ex-spouse on some level. Many refer to this association, in which both of you share the job of raising the children, as an unexpected partnership. It is certainly a different relationship from the one you had when you were married, but it is a relationship nonetheless. Even if you are connected only by financial orders stemming from your divorce, any post-divorce contact can be challenging. You will have to learn how to manage this new form of association, which is not often easy to do and requires effort, patience, and respectful conduct of both parties. Unfortunately, not all ex-spouses act in good faith.

DEALING WITH YOUR EX-SPOUSE

It is fortunate if you and your ex-spouse get along or can at least have a cordial relationship. It makes life a lot easier. Even if this is not the case, however, there are steps you can take to foster a positive connection and minimize conflict. You may not be able to control your ex-spouse, but you can control yourself and the effect interactions with your ex have on you, and any stable ground you can find in this area will be beneficial to you and any children you have.

REGARDING CHILDREN

How you raise your children is of the utmost importance. You and your ex-spouse are partners in this shared task—especially when children move from one house to the other and then back again. In order to give it the best chance of success—i.e., the development of healthy and happy kids—you must communicate with each other frequently, work hard, and work together. This is not an easy job, even if relations are good. Of course, if they are not good, it will take even more effort to accomplish.

Focus on the Children

It usually is best, especially at the beginning of your post-divorce life, to keep communications with your ex-spouse limited to the health, education, and general welfare of your children. No matter the circumstances of your divorce, you and your former spouse likely share a desire to be good parents. This can be the foundation of your new relationship.

Create a System of Communication

Although you may have a solid foundation for your new relationship, you still need to build on it, and creating a decent system of communication with your ex-spouse is a good place to start. Establishing an efficient way of providing each other with information about your children is crucial. Most find that communicating through email or text, especially at the beginning of your post-divorce life, is best. Communicating in this way has several benefits. It provides each spouse a greater chance to think about what to say and, more importantly, how to say it. It also provides a record of what was said. It minimizes in-person interaction, which, for some, can be difficult immediately following a divorce. Phone calls should be used for urgent or time-sensitive matters, such as a health emergency regarding a child or letting the other person know you are running late for an exchange.

The frequency of your communication with your ex will depend on the age of your children and whatever they or you as a parent may be dealing with at any given time. Commonly, younger children will require more communication between parents than older children. For infants and toddlers, it will likely be important for one parent to tell the other what the children ate, when they last ate, when and for how long they may have napped, etc., during pick-up or drop-off exchanges of custody. If any child is on medication, the time it was last administered and its dosage would also need to be provided. Young children often have homework or other school tasks to do, so one parent will have to advise the other as to what may be due the next day or later in the week and ensure that this homework goes with the child and is noted by the other parent.

Adolescents often face emotional issues, which may show up differently in each parent's household. It is suggested that ex-spouses keep each other informed of the emotional issues they may be seeing in their adolescent children and acknowledge that teens may share their feelings and interact differently with each parent. If your co-parent is going through a hard time with your teen, be sure to offer your support. Discuss how best to handle it so that you—the parents—can present a unified front. With younger kids, communication regarding these matters could be daily, while with older kids it could be weekly.

Unless you have sole legal custody of your children or your divorce orders state otherwise, always discuss any major concerns you have regarding the health, education, or general welfare of your children with your ex-spouse. Barring an emergency, this should be done prior to addressing such matters with your children's schools or medical providers. Give your co-parent the opportunity to offer input and participate in any meeting, discussion, or evaluation with any relevant third parties. Don't make professionals have to meet with or obtain information from parents separately. Doing so would not only create undue hardship on these professionals but also possibly cause gaps or inconsistencies in the information these professionals have on your child. Whatever differences you have with your ex, put them aside for the sake of your children.

When communication between parents is too difficult to maintain on their own, there are companies that offer a communication platform that assists with co-parenting. The use of these services replaces the use of texts and emails, which can be lost, hard to follow, or retroactively manipulated. Common providers include *Our Family Wizard*

Keeping Good Records Following a Divorce

Your relationship with your ex-spouse is now more of a legal one than anything else. Your divorce terms are orders of the court. Whether your situation requires you to have a lot of interaction with your ex-spouse or only a little, it is important to keep accurate records. These records can be useful if you need to show that you have complied with court orders or that your ex-spouse has not. (Although your divorce is final, the court has continuing authority to enforce its orders.)

If an ex-spouse fails to comply with court orders, the other may file a motion with the court to have a judge address the matter. If you are required to pay anything, make sure to retain proof of payment. If you are supposed to transfer funds, list a property for sale, hire a professional to divide a retirement account, or engage in any other duty, keep copies of whatever documents that prove you did so. If one party agrees to allow the other to meet a commitment or make a payment later than ordered, put this agreement in writing and retain it. This is especially important if you are the person getting the extension. If the matter goes to court, you don't want a judge to think that you simply didn't follow orders.

It is important to keep records of any communication you have with your ex-spouse of any type—phone calls, emails, texts, letters, etc.—which concern your children or court obligations. Apps such as *Our Family Wizard* and *AppClose* can help ex-spouses to maintain relevant communication records in one place for future reference. Attorneys and judges rely on these communications and other information supplied by parents through these platforms all the time. If you don't share children or utilize these services to communicate and *AppClose*. (See Resources on page 169.) Some charge a fee, while others are free to use. These applications track and save communication records in one place and note when a communication has been opened and read. They feature a shared calendar function that both parents can utilize to import and keep track of important dates for the children, such as school meetings, sports events, recitals, tutoring, doctors' appointments, etc. They also allow the users to log expenses that need to be

> with your ex-spouse, you can still document important interactions in your own way, being mindful to save this documentation and be able to find it if needed. Some people set up separate email accounts for just this purpose. A good practice is to limit individual emails to one topic and list this topic in the reference section of the email. In this way, no one will have to wade through a lot of other "stuff" to address a particular issue. It is also a wise practice to back up these emails, either electronically (in the cloud or on a hard drive) or by printing them out.
>
> Most people today prefer to text rather than email, but texts are a little harder to manage for future use. They are also often not as clear a form of communication as email due to their brevity. Texts that have been sent recently may not contain the date and simply say "yesterday" or "Tuesday," which is often not ideal for court purposes. Saving them usually requires taking a screenshot, emailing it to oneself, and then printing the email. Attorneys and judges who have tried to read a series of texts that has been printed know the task is manageable but not easy. Sometimes it's hard to decipher who is saying what.
>
> As an attorney, I prefer email, but judges understand that texts are common and will accept them as evidence if properly offered. It is in your best interest to be mindful of the shortcomings of texts. Make sure your texts are clear, try to keep threads to one topic, and, if copying and printing them, do so after the full date is shown. Finally, don't use derogatory names for your ex-spouse in your contact settings. It is inappropriate, and introducing a text thread that refers to your ex-spouse in a demeaning manner will not go over well with the judge.

shared. Many divorce orders, in fact, require that one of these services be used, based on the assumption that their use increases the chances of proper communication between parents, minimizes conflict, and provides the court and others with the ability to review or monitor parental communication if necessary.

Follow Through

A shared focus on the children and an effective system of communication are necessary for good co-parenting, but without follow-through they are still insufficient. It is imperative that both parents do what they say they are going to do and what they need to do as co-parents. This creates trust between children and parents, and between ex-spouses. Trust is essential to our overall well-being. It reduces uncertainty and provides a sense of support, allowing us to take on all the other challenges life throws at us.

Get Outside Help

If, despite trying all of the above, difficulties with your ex-spouse are negatively affecting your ability to raise your children together, there are family therapists that may be able to help. They are called *co-parenting counselors* or *co-parenting coordinators*. These specialists are not engaged by you for individual counseling, they are mental health professionals that are trained to assist divorced or unwed parents with the task of co-parenting. (If they think you or your ex-spouse needs individual counseling, however, they may refer you or your ex-spouse to someone else for this service.)

A co-parent counselor, as the name suggests, is employed to help you and your ex-spouse be better co-parents. Use of a co-parent counselor can be by agreement or may be ordered by the court. These professionals often work on parental expectations and communication between parents. They try to identify common goals and align the work of each parent to achieve these goals, building on each parent's strengths. Ex-spouses attend regular meetings with their co-parent counselor together. Ex-spouses learn and try new methods of interacting and then report and discuss the results with their counselor. Work is usually done incrementally, with the hope of building an effective working relationship. The focus is on education and awareness.

Such counseling can last as long as you and your ex-spouse find it helpful and it is recommended by the co-parent counselor. Ideally, you both will "graduate" from such assistance and be able to effectively move forward as a team, using the skills learned. Of course, this does not mean you can never go back. It would be wise to re-engage such services if needed in the future to help with a difficult situation—perhaps in regard to an issue with your child or a new challenge in your co-parent relationship, such as a new significant other or a new family unit. Just as your child grows and evolves, so will your co-parent relationship. It may need occasional maintenance. There is nothing wrong with that.

Sometimes co-parenting fails even with the assistance of a co-parent counselor. These parents usually contact their attorneys and wind up back in court as a result of one or both parties filing post-divorce motions requesting assistance or orders from the judge. If this happens, a co-parent coordinator may be ordered by the court. This intervention is more about providing a way to make timely decisions regarding your children and keeping you out of court rather than finding a way for you and your ex-spouse to work together without professional assistance. The exact process varies by provider and order of the court. In general, parents have a very short time to work out any issues they have regarding their children between themselves. This time period begins with one party giving written notice to the other of the issue and requesting a response. Generally, the required time to reach an agreement can be as short as twenty-four hours or up to two weeks, depending on the issue.

Issues on the shorter end of the time spectrum could include getting consent for a child's summer camp enrollment, vacation dates with a particular parent, or attendance at a school function—things that should not need that much time to consider. Issues on the longer end could include a child's non-emergency medical treatment, academic courses, or requests to begin driver's ed. If there is no agreement within the prescribed timeframe, then one or the other parent—usually the one who brought up the issue—must reach out to the co-parent coordinator to make an appointment within a certain period of time. The parents must then meet with this professional and try to work things out with this person's assistance within a certain period of time.

Failing to reach an agreement usually results in the co-parent coordinator being granted the ability to make the decision regarding the child and provide notice of this decision in writing to the parents. Normally, both parents have to follow the decision unless a disagreeing parent files a motion with the court within a certain period of time. The purpose of the motion would be to have a judge decide the issue after a full hearing. The court will normally be made aware of the decision of the co-parent coordinator at the time of the hearing. The co-parent coordinator may or may not be present to testify at the hearing. If the judge agrees with the decision made by the parent coordinator, the parent who challenged the decision and requested the hearing may have to pay any attorney fees and other costs incurred by the other parent. The parent who challenged the decision may face other negative consequences as well, such as paying for the co-parent coordinator's time.

Will I Still Need My Attorney After My Divorce?

The answer to this question is likely yes. Most divorced spouses still need their attorneys after their divorces. If your divorce requires a trial, then the decision of the judge, which is often received in writing several weeks after the trial, will need to be reviewed with your attorney. You may need the guidance of your attorney to make sure any immediate tasks required by you are undertaken correctly. You will likely have follow-up questions about how to implement some of the financial or child-based terms. After these matters have been taken care of, your need for an attorney should be greatly reduced and may even be eliminated if all orders are followed and no issues arise.

If your ex-spouse does not comply with court orders or you are accused of not doing what you are supposed to do, or if you have a disagreement with your ex-spouse about what the terms of the orders require, then you will likely require assistance from your attorney again. In addition, if either you or your ex-spouse wants to try to change any orders of the court, then you will likely require assistance from your attorney. These matters may be handled and disposed of without the need to return to court (perhaps by talking, writing a letter, or mediation) or they may not.

Usage of a co-parent coordinator is meant to resolve a problem quickly by keeping strict time limits on the process. Its ultimate goal is to prevent—as much as it is possible to do so—the difficult relationship of the parents from holding up a child's life and cease the child's exposure to any more parental conflict. It gives a lot of power to the co-parent coordinator and the process, which some may find excessive. It is likely preferable, however, to having a court rule that joint legal custody is not in the best interest of a child. If this were to happen, then the court might designate one parent as decision maker for the child, thereby eliminating conflict and delay completely. It is best to try to avoid this result by accepting any assistance that is offered and using your best efforts to agree on disputed issues.

> For those who co-parent, post-divorce advice from attorneys is often sought when there is a substantial change in family structure beyond the divorce. Perhaps one parent is moving, about to cohabitate with someone, or getting remarried. Advice from attorneys is also sought when there is a substantial conflict over parenting: a disagreement regarding the education, medical treatment, or living situation of a child. It may also be needed if there are constant issues with co-parenting, such as inappropriate communications with children, pitting a child against a parent, or undermining a parent. These problems can arise shortly after a divorce or over many years following a divorce.
>
> The nature of the issue, how much time has passed since your divorce, and your attorney's practice will all determine how your attorney may be able to assist you. Your attorney may be able to answer a quick question over the phone or through email. It may be necessary to see your attorney in person. In most cases, any substantial new work will require a new retainer agreement and payment. It is important to note that you are not required to go back to the same attorney who represented you in your divorce. If, for any reason, you do not want to continue working with that attorney, you are free to choose another. Obviously, this person will need to become familiar with your case before advising you.

REGARDING FINANCES

If there are no children involved in a divorce, then finances may be your only reason to maintain a connection with your ex-spouse after your divorce. Whether this connection ends up being brief or long lasting, you will have to interact with your ex-spouse in some way during this period. For your sake and the sake of your former partner, try to keep these interactions cordial. Be respectful. If your ex-spouse is late with a payment or hasn't taken an action by a required due date (such as listing a house for sale), reach out in writing. Politely advise your ex that a payment or action is past due and ask if it was simply an oversight or if there might be an issue that needs to be discussed. There might have been an emergency or perhaps a genuine mistake was made. If so, launching into accusations and making derogatory comments will only serve to damage your already strained relationship. Even if your ex has no excuse, it will do you no good to overreact, especially when the way you handle the situation may be documented and shown to a court at a later date.

If an ex-spouse needs a little more time to pay a bill or make an alimony payment, then consider complying if doing so would do no harm. Your ex may have a legitimate reason for being late with a payment. Showing courtesy can go a long way. I've found that those who withhold courtesies find they don't get them when they need them, and those who do not withhold courtesies often (but not always) get the same flexibility in return.

It is important to note that any agreement to deviate from a financial order should be confirmed in writing by both parties. Doing so will minimize the chance of confusion later on if one party happens to forget about the agreement. Notify your attorney of any substantial or ongoing change that you and your ex-spouse have agreed upon, as you will need to be advised on how best to handle this change. It may need to be formalized with the court.

Unless court orders state otherwise, it is usually best for you and your ex-spouse to keep each other informed in a timely manner of any change of addresses or contact information until no further obligations between the two of you remain. This will ensure you receive prompt notice of any required information or payment, and that you will be able to reach your ex-spouse if necessary.

LETTING GO

We can't properly go forward if we keep looking back, right? We are supposed to learn from our pasts, both the good aspects and the bad, and move on. Likewise, spending time and energy trying to change the way someone acts or constantly getting frustrated by someone's actions or inactions is sure to impede our ability to grow, develop our own talents and relationships, and find happiness. Letting go of the desire to do these things is hard. It is much easier to fall into the same old habits and allow old hurts to linger. It takes practice, but, as you learn in the next section, you can let go.

Getting Past the Past

Dwelling on or worrying about the past is not a productive use of your time, nor is it a healthy thing to do. Nevertheless, divorce tends to bring up many questions. Some questions are about the marriage: *Did I try hard enough in the marriage? Should I have left earlier? How could I not have known?* Some questions are about the divorce itself: *Did I make the right decisions during the divorce? Should I have fought harder or not quite as hard for certain divorce orders? Could I have presented my case to the judge better? Did I make the right choice for my kids?* According to discussions I've had with clients and family therapists, these thoughts are common and seem to decline—or are at least better managed—over time. The following advice can help you to manage these worries:

- Acknowledge your feelings but keep them in perspective. In all likelihood, you did the best you could do under the circumstances. If you did not, then make amends where possible and strive to do better going forward. Either way, don't be too hard on yourself.

- Strive to limit self-doubt about the past to a few minutes a day. Allow yourself time to grieve the loss of your marriage and past life, if necessary, then tell yourself that the rest of your day is going to be focused on the present and future.

- Try to forgive your ex-spouse for any actions you feel were inappropriate—even if only to yourself. Forgiving someone can be a difficult task, but time and time again I've been told it brings peace to the person who is able to do it.

Client Tips

I can give you all the advice in the world on how to let go after your divorce but hearing it directly from a few of my clients may be the best way for you to understand the importance of moving on and how to do so.

"I was very stuck on the infidelity part surrounding my divorce. I remember looking through pages and pages of phone and text records of my ex, where it really did nothing but make me more emotional. I should not have spent so much of my time and energy on this."

"Create a vision board as to how you would want your life to look like. You can choose to be sad and dwell in the past, or you can choose to move on with your life and be excited for what is to come."

"I've learned the skill of putting the past behind me. After many, many appearances in court and all the difficulties surrounding that, it was hard to finally let it go when it was all said and done. I literally had to reprogram my brain to move forward and stop thinking about what had happened and what I should or should not have done."

There is a path forward, and you can take it by letting go of the past. Letting go may not be easy to do, but you can do it.

The Things You Cannot Change

The Serenity Prayer is an old and commonly quoted request for peace. It reads as follows:

> *God, grant me the serenity to accept the things I cannot change,*
> *Courage to change the things I can,*
> *And the wisdom to know the difference.*

Why ask for the wisdom to know the difference? Because it is a waste of time to try to change things that cannot be changed—and a source of great suffering. This idea is nothing new, but it bears repeating, especially when you encounter difficulties with your ex-spouse. We humans try so hard to control what seems like the chaos of our lives, and few things feel more chaotic in life than going through a divorce. It is natural to forget our limitations.

We can follow the tips mentioned in this book to try to promote a good post-divorce relationship that minimizes conflict and still be met with resistance. Should this occur, you need to accept it. Prepare yourself for the likelihood that your ex-spouse is going to be difficult and plan on how to handle it. If an ex-spouse is violating the court's orders or acting in such a way as to warrant a change in the custody or parenting plan orders, you need to discuss and pursue the matter with your attorney. You may have to return to court and engage in the legal process again. So be it. Enforcing your rights and protecting your children through legal means may be necessary. Sometimes difficult behavior does not warrant court involvement, but it nevertheless causes strife. The challenge is not to allow your ex-spouse's actions to control you. Here are some tips to assist you in doing so:

- **Get in the right mindset.** Acknowledge that your ex-spouse is going to be difficult. Acknowledge that this is a problem that you cannot control and for which you are not responsible. Acknowledge that you have the option of not engaging in negative behavior. Acknowledge that you will need to take the "high road" in many instances for the benefit of you and your children, and that this effort will be worth it in the long run.

- **Find an outlet.** Find an outlet away from your ex-spouse and your children for any frustration you experience. Acknowledge your right to be upset or disappointed with your ex-spouse's behavior but put a time limit on these feelings. Get your frustration out and spend the rest of your day focusing on the positive aspects of your post-divorce life.

- **Make contingency plans.** If you know your ex-spouse is going to be late with payments or child exchanges, try to have a back-up plan in place, which will minimize stress on your part.

- **Get help.** Obtain assistance from a mental health professional if necessary. Mental health specialists can teach you techniques and coping strategies that will allow you to manage difficult relationships.

EMBRACING THE FUTURE

You're divorced. It took time and a lot of work to get here, and you may be asking yourself, "What now?" Beyond adjusting to your new relationship with your ex and a new schedule with your children, you need to figure out how to navigate the new you. What do you want to do? How do you see your future? Many have a hard time answering these questions at first. Your schedule and daily activities may still seem to be preset routines attached to someone else's wants or needs, but this is actually no longer the case. You undoubtedly have obligations that must be maintained, but you may also begin to look at life through a new lens. Embrace this perspective.

Try Something New

Once you stop letting the past define you, a whole new world of possibilities for personal and professional growth opens up. This applies to everyone. Consider taking up a new hobby or resume one that you once enjoyed but stepped away from. Take a class that interests you—one that will support your career or one that will boost your résumé. Chances are you will meet people with like interests. Get in touch with old acquaintances. Redecorate a room. Experiment with a new fashion or hairstyle. Start new traditions with your children. Visit new places. I'm not suggesting you spend a lot of money or totally change the lifestyle to which you and your children are accustomed. I'm just asking you to be open to positive change and resist the urge to dwell on the past. Small changes and new experiences can boost your confidence and help you and your children to focus on the present and future.

Take Charge

Embracing your future also means taking charge of it. When you were married, chances are that you and your spouse divided the duties involved in managing everyday life. Now it's up to you. Here's a good exercise: Write down all the things you did not do, which may have included:

- managing the finances or paying bills;
- going grocery shopping;

- cooking;
- doing the laundry;
- cleaning;
- taking care of household repairs (either doing the fixing or arranging for repairs);
- taking care of household maintenance (either doing the maintenance or arranging for it to be done);
- scheduling doctors' appointments;
- doing the lawn maintenance or other outdoor maintenance;
- helping the children with their homework or ensuring its completion;
- taking care of the children's school or camp registration;
- getting the children's school supplies;
- planning the summer calendar or vacation;
- managing the children's activities or sports (registration, getting equipment, arranging travel);
- managing the children's religious education or attendance;
- doing the taxes or getting them done; or
- meeting with a financial advisor or financial attorney.

Ideally, you should continue (or start) to divide child-related responsibilities with your ex-spouse. A frank discussion should be had so that both parents are clear on what they are to do or not do. And if the other parent won't help with some or all of the responsibilities, at least you'll know and can plan for this outcome. Remember, planning reduces stress.

Of course, one person can't do everything. Of the remaining responsibilities, pick the ones you will do, the ones you will have to hire others to do, and the ones that might not get done. Identify the professionals you may need in the future to help you based on your list, try to obtain recommendations, and then get the contact information of these professionals. It's better to get this information before you need it, but be sure to remember where you put it!

Regardless of whether or not you were always the one who handled the finances or met with financial professionals in the past, it is wise to consult with someone who can help you prior to and following your divorce. Your financial situation will change, and it's always good practice to review your budget and plan for the future.

Consider your future with an open mind and an open heart. Prepare yourself as much as possible and go forth. You will be surprised at what you are capable of when you allow yourself to try new things with optimism.

CONCLUSION

Being in a position to be able to let go, live your life in relative peace, and not have your happiness be dependent on someone else is a real triumph. Hopefully, the advice found in this chapter will help you to do that.

You have an opportunity to write your next chapter. Divorce is the end of your marriage, not the end of your life. Many see this time as a fresh start and welcome the chance to reevaluate their lives, make some changes, and re-chart their courses. In large part, you have the ability to pick and choose which traditions and pastimes you would like to retain from your past and which you'd like to do differently. You have a chance to create new memories with your children and indulge in a little self-care. Focusing on "what will be" instead of "what was" is the key to moving on successfully.

Conclusion

After many years of representing hundreds of people going through the process of divorce, I am most proud and inspired by the transformation I often see in my clients at the end of their cases. I get to witness people move from being scared and vulnerable to feeling strong and confident. Some of this change comes from knowledge gained. Some of it comes from "going through the fire," so to speak. In the end, however, I think most of it comes from within.

Whether for themselves or for their children, somehow people tend to rise to the occasion and do what needs to be done. It takes time. It takes encouragement. Sometimes it takes lessons learned from mistakes made. Sometimes it takes acceptance of things that cannot be changed. But when it happens, it is wonderful to see. It is always heartwarming to recognize the moment my clients start to rely less on me and my office, (and even the court) and begin making decisions and plans for themselves. It is amazing to watch them let go of the past or their preoccupation with how they ended up where they are. They are no longer victims of circumstance but now masters of their fate.

If you are reading this book, you are probably going through or about to go through the process of divorce. You will go through many stages of worry, concern, and sadness. Depending on your situation, you may also feel cautiously excited. Whatever the case may be, be mindful of how you react to each step in front of you. Know that there are ups and downs to litigation and even mediation. Try to roll with the punches. Don't give up. If you use the recommendations in this book to hire an attorney, mediator, or collaborative team, then you should trust these professionals. Let them guide you and bear some of the burden. And never be afraid to ask questions.

Take care of yourself—and any children you may have. Establish your support system. Create or discover outlets for your stress. Think and plan for your post-divorce life.

I wish you a better future, and I hope the information in this book helps you to get there.

Glossary

This book sometimes uses terms that are common in discussions of divorce but may not be completely familiar to you. You may hear these terms when discussing divorce with attorneys or other law professionals. Definitions are provided below for words that are often used by those who handle divorce cases, all of which are noted by the use of *italic type* in the main text.

alimony. Required monetary payment made to an ex-spouse as financial support. May also be payable to a spouse while a divorce is pending.

arrearage. Amount of child support that is past due.

attorney for minor children (AMC). Attorney who obtains information pertaining to the children involved in a divorce case and then reports it to the court, while also advising the court on what the children would like in regard to the divorce. May also offer an opinion on what outcome might be in the children's best interests.

automatic orders. Court orders that prohibit parties in a divorce from taking any action that would change the couple's current finances or living circumstances until further orders are issued.

bench. Refers to where the judge sits in the courtroom. Also used to refer to a judge or panel of judges.

brief. Written legal support for an attorney's positions. This normally includes a summary of the facts of the case, a list of relevant case or statutory law, an argument portion that connects the law to the facts of the current case, and a conclusion.

closing argument. Reasoning behind why a party's proposed orders should be ordered by a judge. Based heavily on the law and the evidence presented.

collaborative divorce. Non-adversarial divorce option that falls between traditional litigation and mediation.

co-parenting coordinator. Mental health professional trained to assist divorced or unwed parents with dispute resolution services. Engaged in high-conflict cases. Services may involve decision making on the part of the coordinator.

co-parenting counselor. Mental health professional trained to assist divorced or unwed parents with the task of co-parenting between themselves. Focus is on productive child-centered communication between the parents.

court fees. Costs associated with duties performed by a court, such as opening up a file or providing certified copies of legal documents.

court reporter. Individual responsible for recording all that is said at a deposition or during an in-court proceeding.

cross-examination. When an attorney (or party) questions an opposing party or any witnesses of an opposing attorney after direct examination by opposing counsel (or opposing party). This takes place during a legal proceeding, such as a court hearing, trial, or deposition.

defendant. Individual at whom a legal action is aimed. Person who is being sued or charged with a crime.

deposition. A legal proceeding in which a party or witness is required to answer questions in person while under oath. The party or witness may also be required to bring documents to the proceeding.

direct examination. When an attorney (or party) questions their witness during a legal proceeding, such as a court hearing, trial, or deposition.

discovery. Process of gathering and exchanging information that may be relevant during a pending legal case.

family law. Practice area of law that addresses legal disputes and issues regarding marriage, divorce, child custody, and child support.

financial affidavit. Itemized list of a person's income, expenses, assets, and debts, which is signed and notarized by the person completing the document.

flat fee. Fixed amount charged by an attorney for all work, or an agreed amount of work, done on a case.

GLOSSARY

forensic accountant. Accountant who finds and tracks financial transactions and analyzes how money comes in and is used.

full representation. Legal assistance that handles all aspects of a case.

gross income. Total amount of money made before all allowable deductions.

guardian ad litem **(GAL).** Person who obtains information pertaining to the children involved in a divorce case and then reports it to the court, while also offering an opinion on what parenting choices would be in the best interests of the children.

hourly rate. Amount charged by an attorney for one hour of work done on a case.

hybrid fee structure. Fee structure that includes a flat fee for a certain amount of work followed by an hourly rate if more work is necessary.

initial consultation. Initial meeting with an attorney.

interrogatories. List of questions related to your finances, work history, health, and, if applicable, children, as well as the reasons for the breakdown of your marriage.

joint family therapist. Mental health professional who assists spouses with the emotional aspects of the dissolution of their marriage, offers tools to help them communicate effectively, and facilitates a parenting plan if necessary.

joint financial professional. Professional who helps to gather a couple's financial information, assists in completing the financial affidavit, identifies the couple's current financial position, and helps the couple plan for their future financial needs.

joint legal custody. When both parents have the right to be informed of and participate in any major decision affecting the health, education, or welfare of a child.

legal custody. Right to be informed of and participate in any major decision affecting the health, education, or welfare of a child.

limited scope representation. Formal term for partial representation.

lump sum alimony. A fixed amount agreed or ordered to be paid in full in one payment or over the course of a few payments.

marshal fees. Costs associated with duties performed by a marshal.

matrimonial law. Alternative term for family law.

mediation. Non-adversarial method of dispute resolution in which the involved parties discuss and attempt to negotiate a settlement concerning a legal matter with the help of a neutral mediator.

motion. Document filed by a party to a legal proceeding requesting that the court issue a specific order. Will normally contain alleged facts and law to support the request.

negotiation. Back-and-forth exchange of communications, either written or oral, which contain the preferred settlement terms of the parties to a legal action and usually include reasoning to support their positions.

parenting plan. Day-to-day and week-to-week schedule of a child with each parent. Will also normally include holiday and vacation schedules, transportation, communication, and other provisions relevant to the sharing of the care of children.

partial representation. Legal assistance that is limited to specific aspects of a case.

periodic alimony. Money that is ordered to be paid in regular intervals over the course of time. This could be for a fixed period of time or open-ended.

physical custody. Term that refers to where and with whom a child lives.

plaintiff. Person who begins a legal action.

post-majority educational support. Contributions to the cost of a child's education expenses beyond high school that may be ordered by a court in a divorce, custody, or child support proceeding.

premarital assets. Money or property a person has prior to marriage.

present value. The idea that money now is worth more than money in the future.

primary physical custody. Custody arrangement in which the children reside with one parent for a significantly greater amount of time each week/month than they do with the other parent.

proposed orders. Terms a party in a legal case would like the judge to order.

GLOSSARY

rehabilitative alimony. Money paid over a certain amount of time and deemed necessary to allow a previously dependent spouse to gain the education or employment skills necessary to become self-sufficient.

request for admission. Document requiring a party to a legal action to admit or deny the truth of a number of statements contained in the document under oath.

request for production. Document requiring a party to a legal action to provide specific documents or other physical items listed in the document pertaining to a legal matter.

retainer. Amount of money paid in advance to an attorney for future legal fees. Similar to a deposit.

separation agreement. Term often used to describe the written contract agreed upon between spouses that contains all the terms of their divorce.

settlement. Agreement reached between parties in a legal case.

settlement proposal. Letter outlining the basic parenting or financial settlement terms being sought by a party to a legal action sent to the other party.

shared physical custody. Custody arrangement in which the children reside with each parent for equal or near equal amounts of time on a weekly/monthly basis.

sole legal custody. Custody arrangement in which one parent is allowed to make major decisions in regard to the children without the other parent's input.

split physical custody. Custody arrangement in which siblings reside with different parents.

summons and complaint. Legal paperwork that initiates a divorce.

supplemental request. Request to update information or produce additional items.

testimony. Oral statements made under oath during a court proceeding.

trial. Court proceeding in which attorneys or parties present a divorce case to a judge for a decision as to the terms of the divorce and to be granted a divorce by the court.

Resources

Nearly every community in the country provides resources in connection with divorce. For help at the local level, please do an online search using a term such as "divorce resources," "legal aid divorce," or "spousal abuse support" in combination with the name of your town, county, or state to find the appropriate resources available in your community. The following resources are national organizations that can be accessed online.

The information and advice contained in this book are based upon the research and professional experience of the author, but it is important to note that divorce law may vary from state to state. Please be sure to consult a divorce attorney or divorce-related organization in your state for information applicable to your case.

CO-PARENTING

AppClose
Website: https://appclose.com
AppClose is an app designed to facilitate co-parenting.

OurFamilyWizard Knowledge Center Regional Resources
Website: www.ourfamilywizard. com/knowledge-center/regional-resources/united-states/ nationwide-%28us%29
OurFamilyWizard is an app designed to make co-parenting easier to manage.

Its website offers information on divorce and child custody resources by region.

Up to Parents
Website: www.uptoparents.org
Up to Parents is an organization dedicated to helping separated and divorced parents to make their children's transition to this new form of family life as smooth as possible. Its website offers resources for both parents and professionals.

FINDING AN ATTORNEY

American Academy of Matrimonial Lawyers (AAML)
Phone: 312-263-6477
Website: https://aaml.org

The AAML is one of the leading organizations of family law attorneys and serves as a resource for clients, lawyers, judges, educators, and the public. Its website offers a "Find a Lawyer" search engine that can help users find a local attorney.

AVVO
Website: https://www.avvo.com

Avvo is an attorney search website and provides general legal information to help people acquire the legal services they need.

DivorceNet
Website: www.divorcenet.com

DivorceNet provides accurate information on the divorce process, child custody and support, alimony, marital property, and other matters of family law, and can help users acquire a consultation from an expert or find a family law attorney, mediator, or other divorce-related service provider.

FindLaw
Phone: 800-455-4565
Website: www.findlaw.com

FindLaw offers a search engine to help users find a local lawyer according to legal issue or law firm. It also provides information on the state laws of each state in the country.

FINDING A FINANCIAL ANALYST

Institute for Divorce Financial Analysts (IDFA)
Phone: 800-875-1760
Website: https://institutedfa.com

The IDFA is a national organization that certifies financial professionals in the field of divorce according to its established standards. Its website offers a search engine to help users find a local financial professional that has been granted certification as a Certified Divorce Financial Analyst.

FINDING LOCAL HEALTH AND HUMAN SERVICES

211.org
Phone: 211
Website: www.211.org

In many states, individuals and families in need can find the phone numbers of the health and human service agencies and community organizations that can help them by dialing "211."

RESOURCES

FINDING A MARRIAGE OR FAMILY THERAPIST

American Association for Marriage and Family Therapy (AAMFT)
Phone: 703-838-9808
Website: www.aamft.org

The AAMFT is a professional organization for marriage and family therapists. Its website offers a "Find a Therapist" search engine that can help users find a local therapist.

ADDRESSING ABUSE, ADDICTION, OR MENTAL ILLNESS

Al-Anon Family Groups
Phone: 888-425-2666
Website: https://al-anon.org

AlAnon is a mutual support program for people whose lives have been affected by someone else's drinking. By sharing common experiences and applying the Al-Anon principles, families and friends of alcoholics can bring positive changes to their individual situations.

Alcoholics Anonymous
Website: https://www.aa.org

Alcoholics Anonymous is a fellowship of people who come together to solve their drinking problem. Membership is free and open to anyone who wants to achieve sobriety.

National Domestic Violence Hotline
Phone: 800-799-7233
Website: www.thehotline.org

This confidential and anonymous hotline provides crisis intervention, information, and referrals to victims of domestic violence. It is accessible year-round, twenty-four hours a day, seven days a week.

National Rehab Hotline
Phone: 866-210-1303
Website: https://nationalrehabhotline.org

This free hotline is available twenty-four hours a day, every day, year round. Its specialists are there to help those suffering from substance abuse or mental health crises as well as provide guidance to their loved ones.

The Salvation Army
Phone: 800-725-2769
Website: www.salvationarmyusa.org

The Salvation Army offers rehabilitation programs for substance abuse, help for those suffering from domestic abuse, food pantries, and other important services.

VictimConnect Resource Center (VCRC)
Phone: 855-484-2846
Website: https://victimconnect.org

The VictimConnect Resource Center is a referral helpline that allows crime victims to learn about their rights and options in a confidential and compassionate manner. It is open on weekdays to all victims of crime in the United States and its territories via phone, online chat, or text.

ADDRESSING CHILD ABDUCTION

National Center for Missing & Exploited Children (NCMEC)
Phone: 800-843-5678
Website: www.missingkids.org

The National Center for Missing & Exploited Children helps to prevent and resolve cases of family abduction, which may be defined as the wrongful taking or retention of a child by a parent or other family member.

About the Author

Kathy Criscuolo Boufford, Esq., displayed a passion for law early in life. Whether she was participating in the debate team in middle school or taking an international law course in high school, her interest in rules and legal analysis was clear. As a college undergraduate at Saint Anselm College, she enrolled in their Great Books program, which prepared her well for the kind of reading, writing, and thinking that law school would require.

While at Quinnipiac University School of Law, Kathy developed an affinity for the litigation process. To determine what the focus of her practice should be, she took a number of internships and part-time jobs during her school years, working in a jail, court clerk's office, mid-sized insurance defense law firm, and two-attorney general practice law firm. After receiving her law degree, she found that working directly with individuals in a small firm suited her best. Initially, her practice covered a wide range of fields, but it gradually gave way to family law.

Over the years, Kathy has added alternative dispute resolution options (mediation and collaborative divorce) to the litigation services she offers. She is a member of the Connecticut Bar Association, Danbury Bar Association, and Bridgeport Bar Association, as well as the Connecticut Council for Non-Adversarial Divorce. She also holds memberships in the local Chambers of Commerce and Business Network International, which provide her with invaluable resources and professional connections to the benefit of both her and her clients.

Kathy is a partner at the firm of Bellenot & Boufford, LLC, located in Monroe, Connecticut, and a highly sought-after speaker on the subject of family law and divorce. To quote Kathy, "My passion for the legal profession still exists. There is still wonder and learning, but also a practical focus that comes from experience. Providing education through this book is part of that focus."

To learn more, you can visit her firm's website at www.bbesq.com.

Index

Abuse
   getting help, 133–134
   emotional, 133
   physical, 132
Addiction, 135–140
Adult children of divorce, 85–86
Alimony. *See* Financial, alimony.
Arbitration, 126–127
Attorney
   fees, 22–29
   finding a divorce, 9–15
   for minor children (AMC), 80
Automatic orders, 31

Child support, 99–105
Childcare, 6, 146–153
Collaborative divorce
   choosing a team for, 64
   considerations, 64–65
   process of, 62–64
Consultation, initial, 18
   questions to ask at your, 20–22
Contacts, 41
Court, appearing in, 127–130
Custody of children
   child-centric planning, 76–78
   disputes, 79–81
   holidays, 72–73

   hybrid, 82
   legal, 68
      joint, 68
      sole, 81–82
   parenting time
      supervised, 82–83
      suspended, 82–83
   physical, 68–69
      primary, 69–70
      shared, 69, 71
      split, 69, 71
   significant others, 73–76
   vacations, 73
   visitation. *See* Custody of children, parenting time.

Defendant, 17
Deposition, 49
Discovery, 43
Documentation, 32

Email address, 35
Evidence, 39

Family relationships, 6
Family services evaluation, 80–81
Family therapist, joint, 61

Financial
   affidavit, 46, 87–93
   alimony, 105–109
   analysis, 96–98
   child support, 99–105
   concerns, 36–39
   documentation, 44
   orders
      final, 98–99, 154
      temporary, 93–96
   professional, joint, 61–62
   property and debt allocation, 109–112
Flat fee, 25
Forensic accountants, 38
Friends, 7
Funds, accessing, 37

Guardian ad litem (GAL), 80

Hiding assets, 36
Hourly rate, 24
Hybrid fee structure, 28

Interrogatories, 48

Joint accounts, 37

Living arrangements, 5
Long-term planning, 42

Mailing address, 35
Mediation, 52
   benefits of, 55–57
   considerations, 59–61
   process of, 52–54

Mediator
   attorney, 57–59
   choosing a, 58–59
   non-attorney, 57–58
Medical care, 35
Mental illness, 140–143
Money, 4

Negotiation, 113–120

Parenting plans, 69–71
Parenting time. *See* Custody of children, parenting time.
Passwords and electronic information, 34
Photographs, 34
Plaintiff, 17
Private investigator, 41
Property and debt allocation, 109–112

Request
   for admission, 48
   for production, 43
Retainer, 22

Settlement, 120–121
Social media, 39
Special property, 33
Stress, 7
Supplemental request, 46

Trial, 122–130

Visitation. *See* Custody of children, parenting time.

www.ingramcontent.com/pod-product-compliance
Lightning Source LLC
Chambersburg PA
CBHW050313010526
44107CB00055B/2216